A LINDISFARNE BOOK

Explorations of Planetary Culture at the Lindisfarne Conferences

# EARTH'S ANSWER

*Edited by*
Michael Katz
William P. Marsh
Gail Gordon Thompson

**LINDISFARNE BOOKS / HARPER & ROW**

The large figure in the cover design
was adapted by Janet Planet from the Codex Nuttal
of Mexico. It represents the Plumed Serpent,
Quetzalcoatl.

# INTRODUCTION

Hear the voice of the Bard!
Who Present, Past, & Future, sees;
Whose ears have heard
The Holy Word
That walk'd among the ancient trees,
　　　* * *
"O Earth, O Earth, return!
Arise from out the dewy grass;
Night is worn,
And the morn
Rises from the slumberous mass.

"Turn away no more;
Why wilt thou turn away?
The starry floor,
The wat'ry shore,
Is giv'n thee till the break of day."

# EARTH'S ANSWER

Earth rais'd up her head
From the darkness dread & drear.
Her light fled,
Stony dread!
And her locks cover'd with grey despair.
　　　* * *
"Does spring hide its joy
When buds and blossoms grow?
Does the sower
Sow by night,
Or the plowman in darkness plow?

"Break this heavy chain
That does freeze my bones around.
Selfish! vain!
Eternal bane!
That free Love with bondage bound."

from **Songs of Experience** by William Blake

# Foreword

This book is made up of talks given at the 1974 and 1975
Lindisfarne conferences. For ten days in late August the
participants — about fifty people — joined in the life of the
Lindisfarne community at its Fishcove center. Each day began
with a half hour of shared silence in the meditation room,
followed by breakfast and the morning session, consisting of a
presentation, a comment, and discussion. After lunch clusters of
people sat and talked outside the lodge or wandered around the
garden; others went to the beaches or for walks together. At 5:30
everyone gathered again for evening meditation, dinner and
another presentation.

The easy pace was deceptive; as the days passed, the task of
relating the emerging themes to each other became progressively
more difficult. Each person tended to become a champion of
one or the other side of various polarities — self transformation or
social action, rural life or urban life, decentralization or world
governance, tradition or New Age. But community life balanced
the intellectual side of the meetings with elements of ritual and
celebration and, perhaps because of this, a different way of
thinking was made possible. In the end came the recognition of a
process of change so pervasive that one could see beyond
opposing views and catch a glimpse of a new historical horizon.

The Earth is acknowledged in the title of this book as ancient
and future source of the process of change we are living through.
This elusive transformation cannot be seen clearly from any single
viewpoint, but begins to take shape in the many ways in which it
enters the lives and work of individuals such as those represented
in these pages.

# Contents

Russell Schweickart was the Lunar Module Pilot for the Apollo 9 earth-orbital flight in March 1969, during which he made the first space walk without an umbilical. He is now with NASA Headquarters in Washington, D.C., where he works on the Space Shuttle and other projects and maintains his astronaut status.

PART ONE:

THE TRANSFORMATION OF THE INDIVIDUAL

# No Frames, No Boundaries

# 1

## *Russell Schweickart*

I suppose the reason that a nice, down-to-earth astronaut like me is here in a far out group like this is somehow to share an experience which man has now had. In early 1969 I flew on Apollo 9. I'd like now to take all of you on that trip with me, through that experience, because the experience itself has very little meaning if, in fact, it is an experience only for an individual or a small group of individuals isolated from the rest of humanity.

Apollo 9 was to be the first flight of the lunar module, the first time we would take that spacecraft off the ground and expose it to that strange environment to see whether it was ready to do the job. The setting was interesting. In December of 1968, Frank Borman, Jim Lovell and Bill Anders had circled the moon on

Christmas Eve and had read from **Genesis** and other parts of the **Bible,** in a sense to sacramentalize that experience and to transmit somehow what they were experiencing to everyone back on Earth, "the good, green Earth," as Frank called it. And those are people you know. They're not heroes out of books—they're next-door neighbors. Their children and your children play, and they're out there around the moon reading from the **Bible** in a way that you know means a great deal to them. And then the next day comes one of those incredible insights. In the **New York Times Magazine**, Archibald MacLeish writes an essay about the step that humanity has now taken. He writes that somehow things rather suddenly have changed, and man no longer sees himself in the same way that he saw himself before. He sees "the Earth now as it truly is, bright and blue and beautiful in that eternal silence where it floats," and "men as riders on the Earth together, on that bright loveliness in the eternal cold, brothers who know now they are truly brothers." And as you're preparing to go up into space yourself that's a heavy trip, because you realize that it's not just a physical thing you're doing but that there's a good deal more to it. So in all the other preparations you make you somehow incorporate that as well.

All this forms the background for that very, very busy foreground, the foreground that involves simulation after simulation—memorizing all those millions of procedures which are required to save your life and the lives of your fellows if you run into this problem or that problem. You attend an incredible number of meetings, going over procedures and detailed check lists and techniques, thinking of everything that can happen or go wrong, and then deciding what you will do in each case. Hour after hour in classrooms, you struggle to keep awake so that you can understand all those systems that go into the spacecraft and that will keep you alive or will kill you if you don't know what you're doing. You take part in testing the spacecraft, not a simulated one now but the real one, and those tests go on and on, until you feel the spacecraft is going to be worn out before it ever gets a chance to perform up where it was designed to work.

And then finally comes the morning when you get up before dawn. Some people are just starting to come to work. You look out the window, and three or four miles away to the north there is this brilliant, white object standing on its tail with search lights playing on it—and it's somehow a white symbol sitting there on the beach ready for its trip into space. It's the most awe-inspiring thing you've ever seen—beautiful. And you go down the hall and have the last of what seems like an infinite series of physical examinations, you eat breakfast, you go down the hall in the other direction and you put on your suit with the help of all those technicians. You've done it a hundred times before and it's exactly the same, except somehow this morning is a little bit different. And you go down the elevator with your two friends and you get in a transfer van and you go over to the pad and you go up that tower and you look out across that countryside, the sea in one direction and the rest of the country in the other direction. And you realize that all those years and years of work—five years, six years, seven years—have gone for you into this moment. And you are deeply moved.

And then you get into the spacecraft and you jostle around and you joke and play up in the White Room as you're getting in—you put signs on the back of the guy who's helping you get in, so that everybody watching on TV sees these ridiculous signs—all those things. Then you lie there on your back and they close the door and you're right back in a simulator—you've done it a hundred times. And you lie there. During the countdown you may doze off and catch some sleep, waking up when you're called on to take a reading or something. Then they count backwards down to zero and off you go.

Somehow it's anti-climactic. It's much more exciting from the beach, watching it and seeing all that smoke and fire and feeling the power and the concentration of energy that's taking those three people up into space. From the beach you feel that, and it causes your whole soul to oscillate with the throb of that sound. But you're inside now, you're going up, and everything looks very much like it does in a simulation and you've done this a hundred times. The only difference, at least in most cases, is that it's all working correctly. I mean things aren't going wrong now. The dials read what they should read instead of what some joker outside throws in as a problem.

And so you go into space. You're lying on your back, and you can't really see out until the launch escape tower gets jettisoned part way up. Then your window is clear, and as you pitch over, getting near horizontal, you catch the first glimpse out the window of the Earth from space. And it's a beautiful sight. So you make some comment—everybody has to make a comment when he sees the Earth for the first time—and you make your comment and it's duly noted. And then it's to work, because you don't have time to lollygag and look out the window and sight-see, because you're up there in March of 1969 and the goal is to put a man on the moon and get him back to Earth before the end of the decade. So, on with the job.

You get up there in orbit, you separate from the booster, and you turn around to dock with the lunar module. And you have a little problem docking, because a couple of thrusters got shut off inadvertently during launch, and you can't understand why you can't control the vehicle. So there's a moment of panic; you go madly around checking switches, throwing switches, trying anything, until somebody notices a little flag that's the wrong way, and you throw the right switches and you dock. You extract the lunar module and now you have to change orbit, so you go through all those procedures. You take out the check list, you read down the list, you leave nothing to memory. And you change the orbit. You light the main engine of the command module with the lunar module now on the nose for the first time, and you wonder whether maybe it'll break apart, but it doesn't. You were part of the design—you knew it wouldn't, but now you really know. And that first night in orbit you eat, doff your pressure suits, stow them under the couches, climb into the sleeping bags, go to sleep.

Up the next morning, eat breakfast for what it's worth, don the suits. And now you've got a full day of checkout again. You're testing the system that held together the first time you lit the engine, but now you're not just going to light the engine; you're going to wiggle it, testing and stressing and straining that tunnel between the command module and the lunar module to make sure it will really hold together. And again you know it will, but after you've done it now you really know—it did. So you've had a busy day there, and again it's eat, doff the suit (you had put on the suit because the spacecraft might have broken apart and it's hard to live in a vacuum, so, just in case, you do it that way). And you go to bed.

And the next morning it's the same process. You haven't quite gotten enough sleep, but it's up and hurry up because you're late. You eat while you get the suits on, then open up that tunnel and go into the lunar module for the first time. It's an amazing sight out those windows because they're much bigger windows. But again don't stop; you don't have time for that. And so out with the check list and down through that day, checking out all those same systems that you know so well from paper—but now you're there and you're throwing the switch. And you check out the guidance and control system and the navigation system and the communication system and the environmental control system and on and on and on. By the end of the day you're ready for the grand finale—you're going to light up the main engine on the bottom of the lunar module, the engine that will take two of your friends down to the surface of the moon if everything goes right. And you have to demonstrate that that engine will work and that it can also push both the lunar module and the command module around, in case one day that has to be done—little knowing that only the next year that will have to be done to save the lives of three of your friends. And you light off that engine and it works, just the way it did in the simulator. It's amazing. So you go back into the command module and you're a little behind again and you hurry up and eat and take off the suits and get to sleep, because, again, the next day is a big day.

And up the next day and back through the cycle. Today is the day you check out the portable life support system, the back pack that will be used to walk around on the surface of the moon and will allow people to live and operate and work and observe—to be human in that hostile environment. So you put on the suit that morning knowing that you're going to go outside. And you get over in the lunar module and you go through all of those procedures. You check out the portable life support system and everything seems to work, and you strap it on your back and you hook all the hoses and connections and wires and cables and antennae and all those things to your body. And you sever the connection with the spacecraft which has become home to you and switch on this pack you're carrying on your back. You let all of that precious oxygen flow out the door of the lunar module, and now you're living in your own spaceship and you go out the door. And outside on the front porch of the lunar module, you watch the sun rise over the Pacific and it's an incredible sight, beautiful, beautiful sight. But don't look at it, because you really

Russell Schweickart 7

don't have time, you see—you've really got to get moving. That flight plan says you're behind again and you've only got forty-five minutes out there to do all those things you have to do. And so you collect the thermal samples and you start taking the photographs—and then you have a stroke of luck. Across the way in the command module where your friend is standing, also in his space suit, taking pictures of you while you take pictures of him, his camera jams and he has to fix that camera. So you have just a moment to think about what it is you're doing. But then he gets it fixed and off you go again and you're back inside the spacecraft and you know you really need to get moving and get everything back together and taken care of and put away and get the food eaten and the suits off and stowed and get to sleep, because the next day is the big test.

The next day you have to prove that you can rendezvous—that you can take those two spacecraft and separate them by a couple of hundred miles and bring them back together again after four or five hours. One of them doesn't have a heat shield so two of you can't come back home unless you get back together. So you get into the lunar module, which has now become a friend, and you go through all the preparation for that rendezvous and you separate. Except when you get to the end of the stroke on the docking mechanism, it goes clunk and you say, "What was that? That wasn't in the simulation." About the time you're wondering what it was and if maybe discretion is the better part of valor and you ought to go back in and start over, your friend goes clunk and opens up the fingers. And you say, "Well, we'll find out in five hours whether it's all okay." So off you go. And five hours later everything has worked right again. It's been a long five hours and you've gone through a lot of tests, but everything has worked and here you come. You're coming back together again and there's no reunion like that reunion—not only because it's your heat shield out there, which is the only way to get back home, but because that's your friend over there. Dave Scott is your next-door neighbor, but he was never a neighbor like he's a neighbor now. And so you dock, you get back together, and you open the tunnel and there's a reunion that can't be topped. And you get everything done and get back into the command module. And you're tired. You're absolutely exhausted. You haven't had enough sleep. You haven't had a good meal. In fact, you probably haven't eaten that day. And you sit there and you take off your suit.

And now you've got a piece of that lunar module left sticking on the nose of the command module, and you throw a switch and it's gone—there's a piece of you that just floats off. It's a machine; so are we. And it goes away, floats off into the distance, having done its job. And now your thoughts turn to things like a shower and a bed to sleep in and all those things that you realize you haven't been thinking of for those five hectic days that you've just been through. But all that is five days away, because the flight plan says now you show that you can go for ten days—you show you can do the whole mission, the endurance part. So for the next five days, while you're thinking about a steak and a shower and a bed and all those things, you float around the Earth doing other tests.

And now, for the first time, you have a chance to look out that window. And you look out at that incredibly beautiful Earth down below. You reach down into the cabinet alongside the seat and you pull out a world map and play tour guide. You set up the little overlay which has your orbit traces on it on top of the map, and you look ahead to where you're going, what countries you're going to pass over, what sights you're going to see. And while the other guys are busy you say, "Hey, in ten minutes we're going to be over the Mediterranean again and you might want to look out." So you look forward to that. And you go around the world, around and around and around, performing these tests. Every hour and a half you go around the Earth and you look down at it. And finally, after ten days, 151 times around the world, 151 sunrises and sunsets, you turn around and you light the main engine again for the last time, and you slow down just enough to graze that womb of the Earth, the atmosphere.

And down you come into the atmosphere. As you come back in you experience deceleration and it seems as though you're under an incredible pressure. You know that you're experiencing at least four g's, four times the force of gravity, and you say, "Jim, what is it now?" And he says, "Two tenths of a g." By the time you reach four or five g's you begin to realize the burden that man has lived under for millions of years. As you look out the window you see your heat shield trailing out behind you in little bright particles, flaking off, glowing, the whole atmosphere behind you glowing, this glowing sheath sort of cork-screwing back up toward space. And finally you slow down enough so that all of the bright lights outside the window, the fireball that you've been encapsulated in, have now dissipated. And you cross your fingers because all through the flight you've been throwing switches and various pyrotechnic devices, explosive devices that have sealed one fluid from another and one portion of the spacecraft from another, have been going pop or bang or whatever. And you've a couple more of those to go, the ones that control your parachutes. So you throw the next to last switch and it goes pop and the drag chutes come out. And you slow down to a couple of hundred miles an hour, and then you throw one more switch and pop, out go the main chutes, and they work. And you realize that the last explosive device, the last switch that you've had to throw, the last surge of electrons through all the wiring has worked. Now that whole thing is behind you and, splash, you're on the surface of the Atlantic and there are people circling around in helicopters and ships. You're back in humanity again. It's an incredible feeling.

And what's it all meant? You know, will man now after that experience be able to set foot on the moon and return to Earth by 1970? Yes. All of those things that had to work and to be proven have worked and have been proven, and you're that much nearer to that incredible goal of putting man on another planet. Have you opened the door to the future? Have you changed the nature of exploration? Yeah. You've done that. Man will not step back through that door and close it, except perhaps for short periods of time. Are there any practical benefits from it? Yeah. Lots of practical benefits, **ad infinitum**—you get tired of talking about them, but they're there. And they make a big difference in the world; in fact, you're dedicated to them because they will make that difference.

But I think that in some ways there are other benefits which are more significant. I think that you've played a part in changing the concept of man and the nature of life, by redefining a relationship that you have assumed all these years, and not just you, but man, humanity, the whole of history has assumed—that relationship to a planet, which is now changed. And you now know that, because it's a part of your gut, not a part of your head. And you wonder, you marvel that an Archibald MacLeish somehow knew that. How did he know that? That's a miracle.

But up there you go around every hour and a half, time after time after time. And you wake up usually in the mornings, just the way the track of your orbit goes, over the Middle East and over North Africa. As you eat breakfast you look out the window as you're going past, and there's the Mediterranean area, Greece and Rome and North Africa and the Sinai, that whole area. And you realize that in one glance what you're seeing is what was the whole history of man for years—the cradle of civilization. And you go down across North Africa and out over the Indian Ocean and look up at that great subcontinent of India pointed down toward you as you go past it, Ceylon off to the side, then Burma, Southeast Asia, out over the Philippines and up across that monstrous Pacific Ocean, that vast body of water—you've never realized how big that is before. And you finally come up across the coast of California, and you look for those friendly things, Los Angeles and Phoenix and on across to El Paso. And there's Houston, there's home, you know, and you look and sure enough there's the Astrodome—and you identify with that, it's an attachment. And on across New Orleans and then you look down to the south and there's the whole peninsula of Florida laid out. And all the hundreds of hours you've spent flying across that route down in the atmosphere, all that is friendly again. And you go out across the Atlantic Ocean and back across Africa, and you do it again and again and again.

And you identify with Houston and then you identify with Los Angeles and Phoenix and New Orleans. And the next thing you recognize in yourself is that you're identifying with North Africa—you look forward to that, you anticipate it, and there it is. And that whole process of what it is you identify with begins to shift. When you go around the Earth in an hour and a half, you begin to recognize that your identity is with that whole thing. And that makes a change.

You look down there and you can't imagine how many borders and boundaries you cross, again and again and again, and you don't even see them. There you are—hundreds of people in the Mid-East killing each other over some imaginary line that you're not even aware of, that you can't see. And from where you see it, the thing is a whole, and it's so beautiful. You wish you could take one in each hand, one from each side in the various conflicts,

*You can't imagine how many borders and boundaries you cross, again and again and again, and you don't even see them*

Russell Schweickart     11

and say, "Look. Look at it from this perspective. Look at that. What's important?"

And a little later on, your friend, again one of those same neighbors, the person next to you, goes out to the moon. And now he looks back and he sees the Earth not as something big, where he can see the beautiful details, but now he sees the Earth as a small thing out there. And the contrast between that bright blue and white Christmas tree ornament and the black sky, that infinite universe, really comes through, and the size of it, the significance of it. It is so small and so fragile and such a precious little spot in that universe that you can block it out with your thumb, and you realize that on that small spot, that little blue and white thing, is everything that means anything to you—all of history and music and poetry and art and death and birth and love, tears, joy, games, all of it on that little spot out there that you can cover with your thumb. And you realize from that perspective that you've changed, that there's something new there, that the relationship is no longer what it was.

And then you look back on the time you were outside on that EVA and on those few moments that you could take, because a camera malfunctioned, to think about what was happening. And you recall staring out there at the spectacle that went before your eyes, because now you're no longer inside something with a window looking out at a picture. Now you're out there and there are no frames, there are no limits, there are no boundaries. You're really out there, going 25,000 miles an hour, ripping through space, a vacuum. And there's not a sound. There's a silence the depth of which you've never experienced before, and that silence contrasts so markedly with the scenery you're seeing and with the speed with which you know you're moving.

And you think about what you're experiencing and why. Do you deserve this, this fantastic experience? Have you earned this in some way? Are you separated out to be touched by God, to have some special experience that others cannot have? And you know the answer to that is no. There's nothing that you've done that deserves that, that earned that; it's not a special thing for you. You know very well at that moment, and it comes through to you so powerfully, that you're the sensing element for man. You look down and see the surface of that globe that you've lived on all this time, and you know all those people down there and they are like you, they are you—and somehow you represent them. You are up there as the sensing element, that point out on the end, and that's a humbling feeling. It's a feeling that says you have a responsibility. It's not for yourself. The eye that doesn't see doesn't do justice to the body. That's why it's there; that's why you are out there. And somehow you recognize that you're a piece of this total life. And you're out there on that forefront and you have to bring that back somehow. And that becomes a rather special responsibility and it tells you something about your relationship with this thing we call life. So that's a change. That's something new. And when you come back there's a difference in that world now. There's a difference in that relationship between you and that planet and you and all those other forms of life on that planet, because you've had that kind of experience. It's a difference and it's so precious.

And all through this I've used the word "you" because it's not me, it's not Dave Scott, it's not Dick Gordon, Pete Conrad, John Glenn—it's you, it's we. It's life that's had that experience.

I'd like to close now with a poem by e.e. cummings. It's just become a part of me somehow out of all this and I'm not really sure how. He says:

> i thank you God for most this amazing
> day: for the leaping greenly spirits of trees
> and a blue true dream of sky; and for everything
> which is natural which is infinite which is yes

Russell Schweickart     13

Brother David Steindl-Rast was born in Austria and received his Ph.D. in child pyschology at the University of Vienna. A member of the Benedictine Order, he has been active in the ecumenical movement which has brought contemplatives from the great religions together. He currently directs a small contemplative community on a converted lighthouse island in Maine.

and that creates a tremendous challenge for each one of us to become precisely that mystic we are meant to be. Here I'm taking mysticism in the strictest sense as the experience of communion with ultimate reality. All of us are certainly called to experience this communion. And there's no one and never will be anyone and never has been anyone who can experience ultimate reality in the same way in which you can experience it. Therefore, you are called to be that special kind of mystic that only you can be.

Now when I say that this has something to do with the child in us, I mean that there is in the child a longing to find meaning, an openness to meaning which tends to be lost or at least overshadowed by our preoccupation with purposefulness. I should say right at the outset that when I use these two terms, purpose and meaning, I'm by no means playing off purpose against meaning or meaning against purpose. However, in our time and in our culture we are so preoccupied with purpose that one really has to bend backwards and overemphasize the dimension of meaning; otherwise we will be lopsided. So if you find an extra-ordinary amount of emphasis on meaning, it is only to redress the balance.

In the child there is certainly a tremendous curiosity about how things work and a tremendous thrust towards purposefulness, and that is the only thrust that we tend to develop. But there is also a great longing for contemplation which we tend not to develop. The typical circumstance of a child when seen in public these days is one of being dragged along by a long arm, while whoever is dragging the child is saying, "Come on, let's go! We don't have any time. We have to get home (or somewhere else). Don't just stand there. Do something." That's the gist of it. But other cultures, many native American tribes for example, had an entirely different ideal for education: "A well-educated child ought to be able to sit and look when there is nothing to be seen," and "A well-educated child ought to be able to sit and listen when there is nothing to be heard." Now that's very different from our attitude, but it is very congenial to children. That's exactly what they want to do—just stand and look and be totally absorbed in whatever it is that they are looking at or listening to or licking or sucking or playing with in one way or another. And of course we destroy this capacity for openness towards meaning at a very young age; by making them do things and take things in hand, we direct them very exclusively towards the purpose level.

Maybe I should say just a word more about purpose and meaning and the way in which I use these two terms, but I don't want to impose my definitions on you. I'd rather invite you to think about a situation in which you have to carry out a particular purpose and see what the inner dynamics are and then compare this with a situation in which something becomes meaningful to you. When you have to accomplish a particular purpose, the main thing is that you have to take things in hand. If you don't know what it's all about, somebody has to show you the ropes, as we say, so you know how to handle the thing. You have to take things in hand, to handle the matter, to come to grips with the situation, to keep things under control—otherwise you are never quite sure that you are going to accomplish your purpose. All this is very important for dealing with the situation in which a particular purpose has to be accomplished.

Now think of a situation in which something becomes meaningful to you. What is there to grasp? What is there to keep under control? That is not the idea. You will find yourself using expressions in which you are perfectly passive or at least more passive. "Responsive" is really the word, but you are more passive than in a situation in which you are accomplishing a purpose. You will say, "This really did something to me." Now you are not the one that keeps things under control and handles them and manipulates them; instead the experience does something to you. "It really touched me," or if it is very strong, "It hit me over the head!" or, "It swept me off my feet!"—something like that. That's when something becomes meaningful to you. So what really happens is that you give yourself to it, and in that moment, it, whatever it may be, reveals its meaning to you. Again let me stress, this is not an either/or proposition. The two have to go together, but certainly in order to find meaning in our purposeful activities we have to learn to open ourselves, to give ourselves to what we are doing. And that is typically the attitude that the child takes.

Now let me go on to a very important type of experience which Maslow has studied under the heading of the "peak experience," those moments in which meaning reveals itself to us—and we know it. In order to say more about this, it is again necessary that

I don't talk about something that's unrelated to your own experience, particularly since the peak experience in its matter, in its content, is so very evasive. In order to be able to speak about it at all, we'd either have to have a poetry session or a music session or something like that. If we want to have a discussion of it, we can only discuss some structural aspects and leave each one of you to fill in the context on your own. For those of you who may possibly not be familiar with the term or who need a little refresher for your memory, simply think of an experience that, when you think back on it, was a moment of which you could say, ''That kind of thing makes life worth living.'' Or think of the term ''peak experience,'' a very well-chosen term suggesting, for one thing, that it is somewhat elevated above your normal experience. It is a moment in which you are somehow high, or at any rate higher than at other moments. It is a moment, although it may last quite some time; even then that long time, say an hour or so, appears as a moment. It is always experienced as a point in time, just as the peak of a mountain is always a point. Now this may be a high peak or a low peak; the decisive thing is that it comes to a peak.

So as you look over your day or over your life or over any period of time, you see these peaks sticking out, and they are points of an elevated experience, points of an experience of vision, of insight if you want. That is also important to the notion of a peak. When you are up on top of a peak you have a better vision. You can look all around. While you are still going up, part of the vision, part of the horizon is hidden by the peak you are ascending. But once on the peak, you get an insight into meaning; there's a moment in which meaning really touches you. That is the kind of insight that we are speaking about now. It's not finding a solution to a concrete package of problems; it is simply a moment of limitless insight. You are not setting any limits to your insight.

Try to think now of a moment of this kind and make it very concrete, very specific. No generalities will help us here. It doesn't have to be a gigantic peak—they are very rare in one's life. But an anthill is also a peak, so anything that comes to a peak will do for our purposes. So just try and remember very concretely an experience in which something deeply touched you, an experience in which you were somehow elevated above a normal level. I will make a little pause so that I myself can also think of one, and then we will look a little bit into the structure of these experiences. And, if these experiences are, as it appears to me they are, the epitome of the mystical experience, then even in our little anthill-type peak experiences there will have to be found the typical structure of the mystical experience, the typical structure of that child-like openness to meaning—the typical structure of monastic life as I will go on to demonstrate. So please try now and focus on one of those peak experiences...

I said that the content of these experiences is very evasive. You might even have to say, "Gee, nothing really happened." Well, that is a profound insight, because if you allow nothing really to happen, that's the greatest mystical experience. But as you talk about it you will find yourself inclined to use expressions such as, "Oh, I just lost myself. I lost myself when I heard this passage of the music," or, "I just lost myself looking at that little sandpiper running after the waves; as soon as the waves come the sandpiper runs back and then the sandpiper runs after the waves." You lose yourself in such an experience, and after you lose yourself for a little while, you are never quite sure again whether the waves are chasing the sandpiper or whether the sandpiper is chasing the waves or whether anybody is chasing anybody. But something has happened there and you really lost yourself in it.

And then, strangely and paradoxically—and this is exactly what we are aiming at; we are trying to find the paradoxes that must necessarily be in any mystical experience—you find that you would also say that during this experience in which you lost yourself you were for once truly yourself. "That was a moment when I was really myself, more so than at other times. I was just carried away." It's a poetic expression. There are certain things in life that cannot be expressed in any way except poetic expressions, so these expressions also enter into our everyday language. But then you find again the paradox, because about the very same experience of which you say, "I was carried away," you would have to say, "Yes, but at that moment, when I was most carried away, I was more truly in the present than I am at any other time." Like most of us, most of the time I would have to say that I am not really fully present where I am. Instead, I'm forty-nine per cent ahead of myself, just stretching out to what's going to come, and forty-nine per cent behind myself, hanging on to what has already passed. There's hardly any of me left to be really present. Then something comes along that's practically nothing, that little sandpiper or the rain on the roof, that sweeps me off my feet, and for one split second I'm really present where I am. I'm carried away and I'm present where I am. I lost myself and I found myself, truly myself.

I go on to another paradox. I suppose that many of you will have chosen an experience in which you were alone—a moment alone in your room or walking on the beach or out in the woods or maybe on a mountain top. In one of those experiences you find that even though you were alone—and, paradoxically, not so much in spite of being alone, but because of being so truly alone at that moment—you were united with everything and everybody. If there were no other people around with whom you could feel united, you felt united with the trees, if there were any, or with the rocks or with the clouds or with the water or with the stars or with the wind or whatever it was. It felt as if your heart were expanding, as if your being were expanding to embrace everything, as if the barriers were in some way broken down or dissolved and you were one with all. You may check this out by finding in retrospect that you didn't miss any of your friends at the peak of your peak experience. A moment later you may have said, "Gee, I wish that so-and-so could be here and experience this beautiful sunset or could see this or could hear this music." But at the peak of your peak experience, you weren't missing anybody, and the reason is not that you had forgotten them, but that they were there or that you were where they were. Because you were united with all, there was no point in missing anybody. You had reached that center, if you want, of which religious tradition sometimes speaks in which everybody and everything converges.

All right, there is a paradox that when I am most truly alone I'm one with all. You can also turn this around. Some of you may have been thinking of an experience in which part of the peak experience was precisely that you felt one with all in an enormous group of people. Maybe it was a liturgical celebration, maybe a peace march or demonstration, a concert, or a play—some gathering where part of your tremendous enjoyment was that you felt that everybody there was just one heart and one soul and that everybody there was experiencing this same thing. Incidentally, this may not at all be objectively true. You may have been the only one who was really turned on like that, but you experienced it as if everyone were turned on in the same way. But even in this situation we turn the paradox around. When you are most one with all, you are really alone. You are singled out as if that particular word of the speaker (if it's some lecture that turns you on) were addressed to you personally, and you almost blush. "Why is he talking about me? Why is he singling me out?" or "This particular passage of this particular symphony was written for me and it was composed for me and it was performed for me; such a tremendous, lavish performance, and it is all for me, right here." You are singled out; you are perfectly alone. And we come to see that this is no contradiction. When you are really alone you are one with all—even the word "alone" in some way alludes to that. It may just be a mnemonic device to remember this, but there may be more behind it—all one, one with all, truly alone.

I'd like to draw out a third paradox, which in some respects is the most important one, and see again if it checks out with your own experience. When the peak experience hits you or lifts you up or whatever it does to you, in a flash of insight everything makes sense. Now this is a very different thing from laboriously finding the answer to some problem, which is the usual way we think that finally everything could possibly make sense. We think we'll get the answer to this problem, but the moment we have the answer to this problem, several others arise. So we think, okay, we'll follow this other problem up to its end; we believe that we can hand ourselves along from question to answer, new questions arising to the next answer, and to the next answer, and then finally we might arrive at the final answer. But what finally happens is that this chain is a circle and we go around and around and around; the last answer raises the first question and so it goes on.

*The moment you drop the question the answer is there*

In your peak experience, somehow intuitively you become aware of the fact that to find the answer, you have to drop the question. Something knocks you over and for a split second you drop the question, and the moment you drop the question the answer is there. You get the impression that maybe the answer was always trying to get through to you, and the only reason it couldn't get through is that you were so busy asking questions.

Brother David Steindl-Rast      21

Why should this be? Why should this happen in our peak experience? There seems a grotesque disproportion between cause and effect. I was doing nothing but looking at a sandpiper running after the waves and running away from the waves; I was doing nothing but lying awake and listening to the rain drumming on the roof; why should suddenly everything make sense?

There's another way of trying to approach this. You might say, if you really try and check out the experience, that something teases you into saying yes. You see the sandpiper and something in you says a wholehearted yes, or you hear the rain and your whole being says yes to it. It's a special kind of yes; it's an unconditional yes. And the moment you have said an unconditional yes to any part of reality, you have implicitly said yes to everything, not yes to each specific thing, but yes to everything that otherwise you departmentalize into good and bad and black and white and up and down. You are not distinguishing. You just say yes, and all of a sudden this whole thing falls into a pattern, and you have said yes to the whole pattern.

Now if this in any way seems real to you, if there is any response in your heart that says, "Yes, that is something that applies to my own experience," then that is enough to show that each one of us has really experienced at some very important moments of our lives what it is that makes monastic life tick. That is very important, especially in this place called Lindisfarne, this outlandish namesake of a monastery that's been extinct for about a thousand years. That's very important for us, because if there is no connection between me, whoever I may be, and monastic life, then this whole thing is not particularly interesting; but if I can see and appreciate that some of the most important experiences in my life are precisely what is the core of monastic life, that puts me in an entirely different position. And that's exactly what I mean when I speak about the monk in us.

Now I would like to make just a few statements about monastic life. First of all, monastic life is a particular form of life. The monastery is a particular place and a particular environment. It could be called a professional environment, a controlled environment, a laboratory, a workshop. In fact, Saint Benedict's Rule, one of the key documents of our western tradition of monasticism, calls the monastery a workshop. It is a place in which everything is geared towards cultivating that contemplative dimension of which we have been speaking, cultivating that mystical attitude, that openness towards meaning which all of us experience in our peak experiences.

So all of us throughout our lives are in a sense amateurs of the monastic life. The only difference between us and monks is that monks are professionals. But, especially in our time, we know that professionals very often are much less good at whatever they profess to do than amateurs are. Therefore, the more people discover how important the monk in them is, and the more they discover how important the openness towards meaning is, then the more important it becomes that everybody, amateur or professional, has access occasionally to this controlled environment in which he can cultivate the monastic or contemplative dimension of his life.

Now I'll just very briefly pick out these three paradoxes once more and show how they are really what makes monastic life, or religious life as professional religious life, tick.

If anybody has experienced the paradox that when he loses himself he finds himself, then that person has inner access to the very heart of what a life of poverty is meant to be. A life of poverty has only one goal and that is precisely to lose yourself and so find yourself. Everything else that has to do with the life of poverty in all the different monastic traditions, everything else that you may think of as phenomena of poverty (monks have no money, or they have all their money in common and have a lot more money than everybody else, or they must ask permission if they want to use the car, or they are only permitted to have so much money in their pockets, or they are not allowed to touch money and so they have to let other people touch the money...) are just ascetic means to cultivate that seed.

Let's not make the mistake of saying, "I lose myself in order to find myself." That is already turning this whole thing into a purpose matter and that's not it at all. I lose myself and I discover that so I have found myself. And now I spend my life cultivating this seed. What lies between the seed and the harvest is that ascetic effort in many, many different forms according to the different monastic traditions. And the harvest is nothing else but what the seed was, because you never harvest anything but what you sow; that is, you lose yourself and so find yourself—only more so. That's all.

Brother David Steindl-Rast          23

If you take the second paradox, that when I'm truly alone, I'm one with all, and when I'm really one with all, I'm alone, you have the seed of a life of celibacy. Again, what lies between the seed and the harvest is simply ascetic effort that can take many, many different forms. It is just meant to cultivate this seed so that in the end you have precisely that, namely to be one with all and alone. One could make a very good case (but I think someone else ought to do that rather than a monk) that married life is another road towards the same goal of being one with all and truly alone. That means that you are one with yourself, that you are not just half of a pair, but that you are truly alone and so one with all—not only with your partner, but one with all. Marriage is not an egotism for two.

And now the third paradox lies at the root of what we call obedience. The first thing that we think of is that you do what somebody else tells you to do. That's a time-honored and very helpful ascetic means towards the end, but to get stuck in this would be totally wrong and totally fruitless. If it is just a matter of replacing my self-will with somebody else's self-will, I would rather have my own self-will; it is much closer to home. The whole idea is to get beyond self-will altogether, because self-will is the one thing that gets between us and listening. All our questioning, all our frantic looking for solutions, is just an expression of our little self-will over and against the totality. The moment I drop that and give it up, the whole comes through to me and gives itself to me. I'm not so intent on grasping it and grabbing it and holding it when I give myself to it.

Obedience means literally a thorough listening; **ob audire** means to listen thoroughly or, as the Jewish tradition says, "to bare your ear." The ear locks have to be removed so that you can really listen thoroughly. That's obedience in the Old Testament. In many, many forms, in many, many languages, the word for obedience is an intensive form of the word listening—**horchen, ge-horchen; audire, ob-audire;** etc.

In other words, obedience, doing what somebody else tells you, may be used as an ascetic means to get over that self-will, that always having your own ideas and your own little blueprints. It's a means to drop all this and to look at the whole and to praise the whole, as Augustine says. But the decisive thing is to learn to listen, and very often doing somebody else's will can be a hindrance to learning to listen; you just become a marionette pulled on strings. This is very important in the context of finding meaning, the context in which we see the mystical experience. When you find something meaningless you say that it is absurd. But when you say "absurd," you've given yourself away—because the term **absurdus** is the exact opposite to **ob-audiens.** **Absurdus** means absolutely deaf. So if you say something is absurd, you are simply saying, "I am absolutely deaf to what this is going to tell me. The totality is speaking to me and I am absolutely deaf." There is nothing out there that's deaf; you cannot attribute deafness to the source of the sound. You are deaf. You can't hear. So the only alternative that all of us have in any form of life is to replace an absurd attitude with an obedient attitude. It takes a lifetime to get just a little way in this.

What all this boils down to is that there is a lot more to life than just the phenomena. There is a whole dimension of life to which we have to listen with our whole heart, mind-fully as we say. Mindfulness is necessary to find meaning—and the intellect is not the full mind. The intellect, one has to hasten to say, is an extremely important part of our mind, but it isn't the whole mind. What I mean here when I say "mind" is more what the Bible calls the "heart," what many religious traditions call the "heart." The heart is the whole person, not just the seat of our emotions. The kind of heart that we are talking about here is the heart in the sense in which a lover says, "I will give you my heart." That doesn't mean I give you part of myself; it means I give myself to you. So when we speak about wholeheartedness, a wholehearted approach to life, mindfulness, that is the attitude through which alone we give ourselves to meaning.

*Mindfulness is necessary to find meaning— and the intellect is not the full mind*

A technical term that is mostly used in the Catholic tradition and is a good term for this is recollection—to be recollected, to live recollectedly. It means the same thing as mindfulness, wholeheartedness, openness to meaning. Recollectedness is concentration without elimination (that is T.S. Eliot's phrase), a paradox, because concentration normally limits. But if you can accomplish concentration without elimination, if you can combine the attitude of focusing on something and yet being totally open without horizons, then you have accomplished what recollection means. Then you have accomplished what all of monastic life in any of its traditions is after—recollected living, mindful living, deliberate living. Thoreau, when he goes to Walden Pond, says, "I have gone into the woods to live deliberately." That means recollectedly in this sense. There are many forms of monasticism that are not catalogued or recognized as such, and they may be much more important than the others. The decisive thing by which you will recognize monastic life is that it is recollected life, mindful life, wholehearted life. It is through wholehearted living that meaning flows into our lives. That means that while we are engaged in purpose we keep ourselves open enough to let meaning flow into our lives. We don't get stuck in purpose.

It may help us if we see that work in the narrowest sense is closely related to purpose. Work is that kind of activity that aims at a particular purpose, and when that particular purpose is accomplished the work as work ceases. Over against this is play. Play does not aim at any particular purpose. Play has meaning; play is the blossoming forth of meaning. You work until you have accomplished your purpose. You sweep the floor until it is swept. But you don't sing in order to get a song sung—you sing in order to sing. And you don't dance, as Alan Watts pointed out, to get somewhere; you dance in order to dance. It has all its meaning in itself.

Now we tend to think that the opposite of work is leisure. Leisure is not the opposite of work; play is the opposite of work, if you have to have a polarity like that. And leisure is precisely the bridging of this gap between the two. Leisure is precisely work-play or play-work; it is precisely doing your work with the attitude of play. That means putting into your work what is most important about playing, namely, that you do it for its own sake and not only to accomplish a particular purpose. And that means that you have to give it time. Leisure is not a privilege for those who can take time for leisure. Leisure is a virtue. It is the virtue of those who give time to whatever takes time, and give as much time as it deserves, and so work leisurely and find meaning in their work and come fully alive. If we have a strict work mentality we are only half alive. We are like people who only breathe in, and suffocate. It really doesn't make any difference whether you only breathe in or only breathe out; you will suffocate in either case. That is a very good pointer towards the fact that we are not playing off work against play or purpose against meaning. The two have to come together. We have to breathe in and breathe out and so we keep alive. This is really what we are all after and is what all religion must be about—aliveness.

Now, the great question is why we are not more alive. And the answer is one word—fear. One thing is at the root of everything that distorts or destroys life—and that is fear. We are simply afraid to be alive. Why are we afraid to be alive? Because to be alive means giving ourselves and when we really give ourselves, we never know what's going to happen to us.

As long as we keep everything nicely under control, everything's purpose directed, everything's in hand; there's no danger, but no life either. A world in which we could keep everything under control would be so boring that we'd be dead. We'd die of boredom. We experience that in little ways every day. We get scared and we keep things under control, but the moment we really get them under control we get bored. Think of interpersonal relationships: "I got her number; I know how to handle her; I know how to handle him." That's all right to a certain point; it's very reassuring. But then comes the point where it gets totally boring, so we say, "Let's have a little adventure." Now the moment we have adventure we have danger; we have risk. We can't have adventure without risk, and so we open ourselves a little bit. We relax our grip a little bit, and the moment we do that it gets very interesting and adventuresome but also scary. The next thing we know, we're clamming up again and we're trying to get things under control again. So we go back and forth, back and forth, between these two poles all our lives, and that's really what the spiritual life is all about. That's what religion is all about—the fear of losing ourselves and what it is that overcomes that fear.

The thing that overcomes fear is courage. But courage is our contemporary expression for what traditional religion in all its different branches called faith. Let's not use that term faith more often than absolutely necessary because it throws us off. We have wrong notions about faith; we think that faith means believing something. Yes, it does mean believing something. If we really trust in a person, if we really have faith in a friend, that also implies that we are believing some things about that friend. But that is very secondary, and if we get stuck in that we'll never get at the root of faith. That's not what it means. Having faith does not mean subscribing to some dogmas or to some articles of faith

*Why are we afraid to be alive? Because to be alive means giving ourselves and when we really give ourselves, we never know what's going to happen to us*

or anything like that. Faith ultimately is courageous trust in life. The particular form that our religious faith takes depends entirely on the time and the place and the social structure and the cultural forms into which we are born, and there is an infinite variety of these. But the essence of our faith is the same at all times and in all places, and it is the courageous trust in life.

Faith versus fear—that is the key issue of religion. That is also the key of our attitude towards truth. We do know that religion has something to do with truth, but it isn't the truth that we can grab and grasp and take home with us. If we grasp and rigidly hold certain truths, next we will clash with everybody who does not hold those truths. When it comes down to it, everybody holds a different truth; there are as many different truths as there are people around. So if we insist on the truth being something that we must hold, then we are at odds with everybody else in the world. But the real truth that we are after is something that holds us; it holds us when we give ourselves, in those moments when we really open ourselves. There is only one truth and it takes hold of each person in an individual way. There must be an infinite variety of ways in which truth takes hold of all of us because in that variety the unity of truth blossoms forth. And it is beautiful and we must assert it and we must celebrate it. That's what life is and that's what religious life is, but it's giving ourselves to the truth, not taking the truth, grasping the truth, holding the truth. It's only the truth to which we give ourselves that will make us free. The one truth for all of us is that we must have courage to give ourselves to truth. Fear hangs on. Fear always grabs for something. The moment we get fearful, we grasp for something with the reflex of the monkey that grabs for the mother. We have it all deeply in ourselves, genetically, that fear makes us hang on to something. Faith is precisely letting go. Even in religious traditions that may not use the term faith, you will find this essence, namely the letting go.

This is the new situation of global religion in which we find ourselves today. It has finally become clear to us that what is really essential to all the different religions is faith, is this attitude of letting go, this courageous trust in life. That couldn't have become apparent to us much earlier than this, than 1974, because we just did not have the material to compare and to see what other traditions were all about. It took a great amount of comparative religion and the gathering of data to really see and verify this, but by now it has become obvious to a good many people (and it will increasingly become obvious to everybody on this globe) that basically there are only two ways of being religious. The border lines which we thought went between Christians and Buddhists, Buddhists and Hindus, and Moslems and Jews are ultimately irrelevant. They are interesting and very important at a certain level, but when we come to the core of religion, they are irrelevant. There's only one line that goes through, and that goes through in another direction, horizontally. Through all the Buddhists, through all the Hindus, through all the Christians, and incidentally through each one of us, runs the line between the right way of being religious, the only way of being religious, and the wrong way of being religious. That is the line between fear and faith. Fear in its religious expressions takes all sorts of forms. Dogmatism is the most obvious one. Scientism is another one, but it's just a different kind of dogmatism. Fundamentalism is one. Moralism is one, because you hang on to something that you can do—it's what Paul called the law versus grace, or works versus faith. You do something; as long as you can do it you have something under control. You don't have to trust anything; you trust in what you can accomplish and manipulate.

Basically, what it boils down to is that there are only two forms of being religious around in the world anymore. If you'll excuse me I will call one fundamentalist and that's the religion of fear. Obviously in the way in which I use religion, it isn't religion at all, but it's called religion, so let's call it the wrong kind, the monkey religion, the aping religion, the religion of fear. And over against that is the catholic faith, but please let's write catholic with a small ''c'' because the great problem with Catholics is that they aren't catholic enough. There are catholic Buddhists who are much more catholic that the Catholics with a capital ''C'' and there are catholic Jews and there are catholic Hindus and there are catholic Moslems. There are even catholic atheists, but there are also fundamentalist atheists. And that's where the line goes through.

The focus is on meaning in the catholic faith. The focus is on riding the bike, as our friend Paolo said last night, over against the purpose of taking the bike apart. When we take the bike apart, we have to take things in hand, and that's fine. It is very good to see the bike's purpose, to see its working, but it has to be in the context of the whole. When we give ourselves to meaning, we really have to give ourselves, and we know how difficult it is for us to give ourselves. If you don't know it just watch your language and see how many, many times a day you use idiomatic expressions in English that say, "I take this" and "I take that." We have not one idiomatic expression that says "I give myself to something." We take a course and we take an exam and we take a walk and we take a pill and we take a meal and we take a shower and we take a bath and we take a seat and we take all sorts of things that nobody can even take—a husband, a wife, a nap. (If you have ever tried to take a nap it's perhaps the surest road to insomnia, but the moment you give yourself to the nap, you're asleep.)

This is the reason there have to be places like Lindisfarne in which we learn to give ourselves as we take things in hand. Lindisfarne, or Houses of Prayer, or other places like this today are trying to become monastic and catholic, but they have a long way to go to become truly monastic and truly catholic. Every one of us has a long way to go.

But we have come a long way because our global consciousness is at this moment saturated with precisely the awareness that what really matters is meaning. When we were children we used to hang a little string into a salt solution and watch the crystals grow on it; no matter how saturated the solution was, the crystals would not grow without the little string. Now Lindisfarne may not be much more than a little string, but it's hanging in the right solution, and what is crystallizing for each one of us personally is the monk in us, and for all of us, global religion.

Pir Vilayat Inayat Khan, son of the Sufi Master and musician, Hazrat Inayat Khan, studied comparative religion and philosophy at Oxford and the Sorbonne under Bertrand Russell and Wittgenstein. He is an accomplished musician, having studied the cello with Pablo Casals. He is the leader of the Sufi Chisti Order and the director of various Sufi communities and study groups in America, India and Europe.

# Walk Without Feet, Fly Without Wings,

# 3  Think Without Mind

## *Pir Vilayat Inayat Khan*

There's no doubt that the whole history of the world is the history of the advance of consciousness. I think it was Aldous Huxley who said that man is the spearhead of the advance of consciousness on the planet, and it's clear from the findings of Reverend Pierre Teilhard de Chardin that consciousness keeps pushing forward through matter and mind. I think what is meant by the advent of the New Age is the great breakthrough of consciousness occurring in our time. My father, Hazrat Inayat Khan, says that humanity is beginning to be conscious of itself as being a being, which means that the individual fragments of humanity are beginning to reach beyond themselves. We have emerged from a very highly individualized culture where competition was foremost. Now there is a reaction, particularly amongst youth, against the sheer brutality that a high sense of individualization engenders. I sense that the meaning of love is beginning to grow much stronger amongst beings who realize the complete fiasco brought about by competition. Some of the communes (we now have one too) are experiments in finding new ways of living which can replace competition with cooperation.

It seems to be a trend that each part of humanity is trying to discover every other part of humanity. For example, the Indians and Europeans who bring their religion to the West or to America often become more Hindu than the Hindus or more Muslim than the Muslims and accept dogmatic restrictions in their way of thinking which they wouldn't have accepted in their own culture. This behavior, a paradox of our time, is simply an indication that humanity is welding itself into a whole and that every part of humanity has to start experiencing osmosis with every other part. Those involved in this process are pioneers in the consciousness of the New Age.

Maybe one of the great events of our time is the sudden discovery of the meaningfulness of meditation. Meditation has an impact on the thinking of many people in our time because it carries one beyond the individual vantage point of consciousness. In Western Civilization consciousness is highly focalized, and the quest for material well-being tends even further to individualize consciousness. For example, just experience yourself sitting quietly in a room listening to a sound in the street. The very fact of wishing to hear what's happening in the street tends to draw your consciousness into a center. If you resist the gravity pull of the perception, then you may experience what I call a buoyancy action or lifting action or de-centering action upon consciousness. In the experiences of the rishis or dervishes, the sense of me as a special person, as an ego-consciousness, has been obliterated. Consciousness thus transformed is able to see things panoramically instead of statically.

For example, our thinking is very much caught up in time because, as Buddha said, we have been lured by desire into a prison. Our prison is really created by our thinking that we are the persons we think ourselves instead of experiencing ourselves in our eternal being. Part of our prison is also created by our having forgotten what we are—forgotten that we are the visitors on planet Earth. We've forgotten our eternal being and just find ourselves caught up in the immediate environment and think of ourselves as that man walking in New York or that lady pushing a pram. She and he think and are even quite convinced they're walking in New York. If they could only watch their bodies walking and realize how extraordinary it is that one is able to make these lumps of flesh start moving. One of the premises of meditation is that something happens to consciousness when it dis-identifies itself with the vehicle through which it functions.

A second premise is that it is possible to watch the mind. If you identify yourself as a person who thinks, you become caught in your thoughts and can't see the wood for the trees. But watching your mind thinking really frees you from that prison. You can then think, well, the mind is made in such a way that it couldn't possibly think otherwise, because that's the way minds are made, just as my body couldn't digest differently from the way it digests, because that's the way bodies are made. Instead of taking your mind, your opinion, seriously you realize that your opinion is your prison. Imagine a man born in the islands somewhere who never came in contact with any other person. You tell him that the earth turns around the sun and he'll say, "Don't tell me that. I **know** that the sun turns around the earth." Most of us get so convinced and so conceited about our opinions that we become imprisoned by them. Sometimes when people start discussing an idea, everybody at once wants to be right. It's like a discussion with blind people who don't realize how they have been caught up simply in the apparent. That is the meaning of Maya. Maya doesn't mean that the physical world doesn't exist. Any statement about the reality or not-reality of matter is also opinion. The theories of Maya, again opinion, are not important. Do you believe in flying saucers, or do you not believe in flying saucers? Do I believe in flying saucers? My opinion and your opinion are not important. What is important is that consciousness is able to break through the limitations of the viewpoint of the individual. This breakthrough is the goal of all scientific theories. The original Greek for the word theory was **theoria**, which means vision, the vision of the being who breaks through the limitations of his thinking. That's why the Sufi says that the man of God walks without feet and flies without wings and thinks without a mind.

*Your opinion
is your prison*

I am talking about a kind of understanding different from the understanding of the individual mind. Some people call it intuition or transcendental understanding. The word "transcendental," which Maharishi Mahesh Yogi used, isn't a bad word at all. Meditation is transcendental. It reaches beyond the limitation of ordinary thinking. Ouspensky said that syllogistic logic is a chapter in logic; there are other conceivable ways of reasoning. In school you learn all about Euclidean geometry and then when you go to university they say, "Oh, yes, parallel lines do meet." Just as Euclidean geometry applies within limits, thinking also applies within limits when it comes to seeing (as Hazrat Inayat Khan says) the cause behind the cause behind the cause.

The dervish always says, "Oh, I am so overwhelmed, I am shattered, the mind is blown." That's a very good term. One could say even that the soul is blown by the encounter with reality. Do you have the courage to look into the sun? Plotinus said one day, "To look into the sun, you have to have eyes like the sun." There are rishis in India who look into that bright sun from morning until evening without blinking. If most people looked into the sun for more than a few seconds, their retinas woud be completely burned. Rumi says, "If I could ever reveal the secret of my love, the world would be in flames." We content ourselves with our petty emotions instead of facing the cosmic dimensions of cosmic emotion. The rishi, the dervish is the one who has had the courage to face divine love; his emotions then seem unimportant in comparison with the meaningfulness that he has discovered in his love relationship with God. Our ignorance is a protection against that which we are not strong enough to know. That's why we are content in our relative thinking, because all the things that we believe in would be shattered if we faced reality. It's much safer to live in one's little concepts; it's much safer to live in comfortable houses. The great beings go out into the storm or go out into the nothingness. To be a spaceman takes a lot of courage. And to be a rishi who sits there in the hills for ten years without seeing another human being also takes a lot of courage. When I was a young boy, in 1936, long before the Spanish Revolution, I was studying cello as a pupil of Pablo Casals, who lived in San Vicente. There were a lot of tourists on the beach but you never saw Pablo Casals. When there was a

The Transformation of the Individual

storm, no tourists, but sure enough, there was Pablo Casals. The unwillingness of great beings to let themselves be shut in or to compromise accounts for the greatness of the rishis and the dervishes whom I have come across in my life.

I don't advocate leaving the world in order to live as an ascetic. It's very important to be able to bring spirituality into everyday life. It's very challenging to be able to be involved and yet be free, to involve yourself with people, but not bind them or yourself. It's very difficult in terms of practical life, very difficult. Suppose that, as a businessman, you've signed a contract, and because of that contract you're no longer able to act according to your conscience. A small being will say, "Well, I'm bound by my contract and that's it." A great being will say, "All right, I'd rather lose the million dollars, but I must have my head high." That makes the difference between the being who's really committed to the spiritual ideal and the man who makes a compromise with matter.

I don't advocate giving up achievement. I think that if one gives up achieving something in life because one feels that it's not worthwhile, it's like saying that the grapes are sour because one is too lazy to go and pick them. One has to know how to introduce renunciation into activity, as the **Bhagavad Gita** says, to renounce the fruit of action. For example, imagine you've worked all your life to build yourself a wonderful house and swimming pool and all the rest of it, and, having reached this point, you give up your house to be used as a home for retarded children, and you live in a little hut in the woods. The beauty of that house will be transferred into your being. My father tells a story of a dervish in Hyderabad who was walking in the streets, probably dressed in rags, and laughing his head off. He turned towards some passers-by and said, "You there," and he told them all about themselves and he looked at other people and said, "And you there," and he told them all about themselves in every detail. How did he know? Because he had lost himself. He didn't know who he was, where he was going, what he was doing and so he knew all about everybody else. The one who thinks he knows all about himself knows neither about himself nor about anybody else. I am talking about a transcendental knowledge that is really **the** knowledge of knowledges.

For example, we would so like to know why things happen the

way they do. Why do I have to meet this person? What do I have to fulfill in my karmic relationship with this person? Why does this event happen to me? Is there really planning, programming behind all things or not? We admire the capillaries in the wings of a butterfly because every capillary has been so carefully planned. It is extraordinary how nature has planned every living thing. But when it comes to our lives, we can't be very objective. We think everything else has been planned, but when it comes to our lives something broke down in the planning. And it is purely because we fail to see the cause behind the cause. Maybe we see what's happening, maybe we don't; but even when we see what's happening, we perhaps don't see why it's happening. Why is it? Why do I have to meet this problem? What is it trying to tell me, or is it just an accident? If it's an accident, then we don't believe that everything makes sense. That is the real metaphysical anxiety of Heidegger. He felt the despair of a soul who is unable to see the sense that things make. That's what used to be translated in terms of believing or not believing in God.

There's a difference between God and my concept of God. There's a difference between the Mont Blanc and my concept of the Mont Blanc. What is my concept of the Mont Blanc in comparison with the Mont Blanc? So what can my concept of God be in comparison with God? It's just an intuition, an understanding that cannot be limited to the rational mind. For example, I have an intuition of being part of a totality. It would be very difficult for me to try to assess what the cells of my body imagine or understand. But suppose one cell of my body were aware that it is part of the whole body. Now that would be something like what happens to the human being when he is aware of God. It's an awareness of the totality of which he is a fragment. It is an intuition. Now you could think of that totality as being the totality of the physical universe, if that's all that you believe in. But obviously, this is another consequence of a limitation of our understanding. If, at a particular moment, we are tuned in to physical reality we assume that it is the only possible reality. In meditation one is conscious of the fact that the physical reality is a condition of reality as, for example, ice is a condition of water. It's as if physical matter were the crystallization of a symphony of light.

*We think everything else has been planned, but when it comes to our lives something broke down in the planning*

Can you remember what physical reality is like when you are dreaming? You generally assume when you wake up from a dream that the dream was unreal and that what is here is real. You may remember something of the impressions of the dream, but do you remember what the physical world seemed like to you when you were dreaming? You felt you were awake and your memories of the physical world seemed like dreams. I am talking only about the dream state, but there are higher states of consciousness in the dream. For example, in a deep sleep, where there are no longer images but there is an intense consciousness, in that consciousness one is aware of having dreamt. One is aware of having awakened from the world of dreams, and one realizes that dreams were the projections of creative imagination. One explains one's self as pure luminous consciousness. There is a form of Yoga called Nidra Yoga which consists of maintaining the continuity of consciousness right into deep sleep. It's as if you are able to look behind a scene of life and you see the reality behind the physical reality.

The whole attitude of the Sufi dervishes is less the desire to know than the effect of being very deeply moved by the discovery of the divine presence and the shattering of the self by the divine presence. As a consequence one's way of looking upon things is altered. Some say that love is blind, that if you love you don't see the person as he really is. It's really the other way around. You can see much deeper into the real being of the person if you are in love with that being. And so, through this divine love that the Sufis talk about, they are able to discover the reality behind the appearance of things. They speak about a world of attributes. For example, if people who are caught up in the individual consciousness come across a very peaceful person, they say, "How nice to meet this peaceful person. He's so peaceful." But the Sufi says, "Isn't it wonderful to discover divine peace manifesting in this person." The person is, let us say, the donkey who's carrying peace on his back. So actually the Sufi is discovering something behind reality. What he's discovering is peace or joy or power or whatever. Yet in fact he's discovering God, not as the totality of which he is a part because that's just the first dimension of God Realization, but as the archetype of which he is an exemplar. That's yet another dimension of relationship. Another example of an archetypal discovery would be discovering that there is rose-ness behind all the roses of the world. That's what Plato means by the world of Eidos, the world of ideas.

The Sufi is continually discovering meaningfulness, first in the form of the bountiful descent of all the many-splendored, divine attributes both within and outside himself. The process includes self-discovery. One of our main concerns is the purpose of our lives. What is the purpose of a flower? To unfold the potentialities contained within it. What is the purpose of my life? Well, can I ever understand it? The purpose of life, says Hazrat Inayat Khan, is like the horizon: the further I advance, the further it recedes. So at first, it seems to me that my purpose is, indeed, the unfoldment of the potentialities of my being. Then I discover that in order to be able to unfold that which is within me, I have to be able to see it in another. There may be great peace in me, but I can't be peaceful until I've come across either a peaceful person or that wonderful quiet brook of clear water that is trickling in the sun high up in the mountains. I experience the peace of my soul looking at that water. Or perhaps I have radiance in me, but I can't really manifest the radiance of my being until I have come across that wonderful sunrise with all those wonderful colors and the sun breaking through in the maze of splendor. I enjoy it so much, and then I discover that the reason I enjoy it is that it helps me to discover myself. I had it in me but I didn't know it. Once a long time ago I met a rishi who said, "Why have you come so far to see what you should be?" Now I realize that in order to become what one is, one has to be able to see it. And so when you are beginning to discover the archetypes behind all things, it helps you to discover yourself, because you are those things that you are looking upon, though at first they would seem to be other than yourself.

But your self-discovery must come out of love and not out of a desire to unfold yourself, for that desire would stand in the way of your unfoldment. Modern psychology is motivated by a desire to improve the individual, but it is oriented toward the expression of individual egotism instead of toward the expression of love. We are beginning to understand that in the New Age we will have to revise our whole approach to things. You don't get anywhere if you start with the point of view of the individual because you've started from the wrong premise. People would like to understand

*Modern psychology is motivated by the desire to improve the individual, but it is oriented toward the expression of individual egotism instead of the expression of love*

The Transformation of the Individual

their purpose, but their purpose only makes sense in terms of a greater purpose. The same principle is true in meditation. A lot of people would like to experience high states of consciousness, and it's that very will to experience them that stands in the way of the experience, whereas if you let a higher will take over from your will or a higher love take over from your love, if you allow an action to be performed upon you, then as Halaj the great Sufi says, you become the instrument of the divine operation. One lends oneself to the divine operation instead of trying to interfere with it. Yet one has to prepare an altar before one officiates at the altar; the wise virgins had to get the oil ready before the lamp could be lit. So one has to be doing something, perhaps even just sitting still in an asana, as they say in Yoga. There are certain things you can do, but, having done them, you have to let something greater take over from you.

In the time of early Hinduism and, later on, Buddhism, there was a quest for liberation, **moksha**, based on the assumption that life on earth is undesirable because, as I said, one lets oneself be caught in a kind of prison. A great soul will always try to burst the walls of his prison and be free. We're not free in our thinking because we are conditioned by the thinking of society. The rishis sought freedom and they realized that it is attachment that binds one and desire that holds one. They tried to free themselves from any form of conditioning whatsoever in order to follow the path of liberation. Buddha was motivated less by this desire for liberation than by wanting to find the cause behind the cause behind the cause. He was perhaps one of the greatest scientists ever in the history of the world. What is this causal chain that involves people in the process of becoming? If you know how to unbecome, you can then become. You can then involve yourself freely instead of being involved because of karma. That's why Buddha said that once you are liberated, you can then return in order to liberate others. Still, behind the whole quest, there has been a deprecation of the meaning of life on the physical plane.

In the Judaic and Christian and Islamic religions, on the contrary, there is an accent on incarnation and, especially in Christianity, on resurrection. If conditions on the earth are simply transient, and if whatever we experience is lost, then what's the point of it all? Why not just free oneself and enter into a state of samadhi? But if the experience of the earth has value, the idea of resurrection offers protection against the destruction and loss of that experience. Then we can understand that resurrection means the distillation of the essence of the essence of the essence of what one was in one's personality, so that all aspects of the personality may disintegrate, and one may survive just as the essence of the essence of the essence of what one was on the physical plane.

We normally identify ourselves with our transient personalities. The personality is considered by the Sufis like a plant unfolding or deploying or unfurling what is contained in the grain, the seed. There is much more in the seed than there is in the plant. The plant may not receive enough water and may not grow very much. All the possibilities of mutation are already contained within the seed, but you can't see them in the plant. The plant can only manifest a small aspect of the richness of the reality of the seed. In the same way, your personality manifests only a very small part of the richness of your being. As long as you identify yourself with your personality, you limit yourself to that part of the seed which has so far manifested in the plant. But if you identify yourself with the seed, then you bring into the plant all the richness that is in the seed. The Realization of the Divine in you will enable you to manifest on earth all the richness contained within your being. According to the Sufi, man's purpose on earth is to make God a reality, to give expression on the physical plane to what is potential but as yet unmanifest. The personality, having incarnated, comes into contact with other personalities and an osmosis takes place. Some richness accrues to the soul for having incarnated on the earth plane; otherwise, there would be no purpose. The seed is eternal but not permanent and unchanging because it is enriched by what happens on the earth plane. The transcendental God is becoming a reality on the physical plane. Neferi, a great dervish among the Sufis, said, "Why do you look for God up there?"

In the beginning I spoke of God Realization as the intuition that you are part of a totality. Then I said it is the intuition that you are the exemplar of a model, or an archetype. Now I say it's the experience of a presence and you are part of that presence. God is born in our midst by our Realization of His Being. Such is the purpose of our lives.

*Richard Baker-roshi has been Abbot of San Francisco Zen Center since 1970, succeeding his teacher, Shunryu Suzuki-roshi.*

# 4 Sangha-Community

## *Richard Baker-roshi*

Individuals and the state have an identity in America, but all other associations are seen as limited to a particular purpose such as business, education, fraternity, athletics, research, worship, and so forth. Community is not seen as a fundamental expression of personal and social identity. And community is not simply an amplification or extension of personal identity; it is an identity in itself, an identity that is more than and other than the individual alone plus other people. Community is certainly a more real and functioning identity than the political, economic and trade unit called the state. The state is primarily defined by its extent and its control of transportation and resources, and very little defined by the emotional and psychological needs of individuals. The state is threatened by real bonding in communities and particularly threatened by any community approaching self-sufficiency or autonomy. (In pre-modern Japan the military dictatorship consciously tried to wipe out the economically nearly self-sufficient small cross-village units called **buraku** by getting their members into debt—tempting them with Tokyo goods not produced by their household and village economy.)

Zen Center is a traditional and innovative Zen Buddhist community that is not exactly similar to any Buddhist community in Japan, China, or Tibet. At the same time Zen Center is a direct descendant of a tradition of meditation and communal life that goes back more than 2500 years to Buddha's own way of life with his disciples, and back more than 1200 years to the specific ways and rules of Zen communal life begun by Pai-chang (Hyakujo) in the 8th century. (His most famous statement was, "A day of no work is a day of no eating.")

Zen meditation is called zazen. Za means sitting, and Zen means that concentration or absorption in which you are one with everything, in which there is no subject-object distinction. Shunryu Suzuki-roshi, my teacher, came from Japan in 1959. He never started a group, but he meditated every day and people just began to join him in meditation. In those early days when there was no community, we thought only one or two people might practice successfully for a long period of time. That it was actually possible or feasible to make a lifetime commitment to Zen practice had not occurred to us. We felt lucky to imagine that we could practice even for a short time, especially since it always seemed imminent that Suzuki-roshi would have to return to Japan. Also, the economic and material circumstances that would permit us to practice for a long period of time were not available, or seemed not to be available.

However, soon there were many people staying a year or two or longer. Then with the starting of Tassajara Zen Mountain Center in 1967, the number of students who were staying a long time and who had an actual feeling for and understanding of Zen practice dramatically increased. In fact, now we find we have to limit the number of students in order to maintain our goal of remaining a face-to-face community of about two hundred residents in our three locations of San Francisco, Green Gulch, and Tassajara. In addition to the residents there are about a hundred more students who live in apartments near Zen Center in the city and a few who live near Green Gulch Farm and Tassajara. There are many more people who come to the public lectures in San Francisco and Green Gulch. Beyond these people in the Bay Area, there are quite a few thousand people throughout the country who correspond with us, or who come to Zen Center as students for various lengths of time, or who come to the summer guest season at Tassajara. So the size of the extended Zen Center community is quite large and varied.

Let me define Zen Center more clearly and establish some of the vocabulary for this talk. Zen Center is a practice and study center in three locations. In San Francisco there is a public meditation hall; a seminary, the Shunryu Suzuki Study Center; and a neighborhood community and service center, The Neighborhood Foundation. In the mountains near Carmel and Big Sur is Zen Mountain Center at Tassajara Springs, the most well-known part of Zen Center. It is a traditional Chinese-Japanese style Zen monastery with a four-month summer guest season open to the public. In Marin County, just north of the Golden Gate Bridge, near Muir Woods and the town of Muir Beach, is Green Gulch Farm. At the farm are a public meditation hall, a large hand-and-horse-cultivated produce and egg farm, beginning experiments in alternative energy systems, and a meeting and retreat center called The Wheelwright Center. Zen Center also includes the Green Gulch Greengrocer, a produce and neighborhood store in the city; the Tassajara Bread Bakery, a general bakery, pastry, and coffee shop in the city; and the Alaya Storehouse, a factory and store where we make and sell clothes, cushions, and mats for meditation and comfort.

While the number of residents is a little under two hundred, the immediate Zen Center community is about 250 persons who have been together for many years—the average is over seven years, and some people have been with Zen Center eighteen years. This cumulative experience in how to live and do things together makes possible everything we do. Faced with our gathering community and the increasing number of married couples and children, in the mid-to-late 60's we concluded that we were not a transient student body but a commmunity (with tenure and stability) that we must recognize and make (its existence and support) an integral part of our practice.

Although Zen Center is a community, it is a practice community and not primarily a residential community. In a Buddhist practice-community, a Sangha, you leave if you stop practicing, while in a residential community, it is residence and not practice that establishes your participation. Exceptions can be made for a person to experiment with stopping practice for a time or for one member of a couple not to practice, but usually if you stop practicing meditation you leave. A Buddhist community or Sangha is not society at large, so it can exclude people. It does not need prisons. A large part of early Buddhist literature details this communal process of how and on what grounds someone not practicing or disturbing the community life and practice is excluded.

Buddha, Dharma, and Sangha are called the Three Treasures of Buddhism. Throughout history people have found the world undependable, painful, and full of suffering, so in Buddhism it is said that we should not take refuge in this conditioned world of suffering; instead we should take refuge in the unconditioned Buddha, Dharma, and Sangha. Buddha is understood as your identity or oneness with the truth. Dharma is the phenomenal world or form itself as the teaching, or your oneness with all things. Sangha is your identity with all being. In a limited communal sense, Sangha means those who acknowledge this identity and make their life intention and work the enlightenment of all beings.

Implicit in the idea and practice of Sangha is that the prevailing society of every period of history will be to some degree corrupt, misguided, or chaotic; and that the antidote to this, the fundamental social action, the only hope, is the maintenance of a tradition that produces realized, enlightened, radically sane individuals. Society needs the presence and companionship of such individuals and of groups of people trying to live this way—people who are trying to find as their first priority the optimum way to live together. In this sense Sangha is a kind of potential or capacity of society to live together—if a few people can find a way to live together, then many people can find a way to live together. At least we ought to throw our shoulders to the wheel.

It is this effort and example, not really the scale of its success, that opens and allows a society to breathe and deepen its expression, singly and together. A community can help us become free from viewing our lives as dramas of success or failure requiring a leading actor and a series of emotional scenes. A community can give us the space and support to express ourselves individually and with others in the simplest, most continuous and adequate way.

The Buddhist Sangha is one of the oldest continuing institutions in the world. It is not local or limited to any particular age, country, or century. So a Buddhist community usually has a very open and precise feeling. Everything does not have to be done in one generation. This large-scale and open-ended time frame is exceedingly important. People need a scale of time and history that allows them to understand how things happen, allows them to feel their own lives continuing and to see the lives of those around them as understandable and accessible. Without an accessible, understandable scale there is likely to be a build-up of frustration, oppression, and social violence.

Culture is produced by people living and doing things together, so the intensity, interactions, and time scale of people living together in a community are extremely potent. This also means that a community must have the capacity and sophistication to absorb, widen, and extend the development of its members who by living together change and themselves become more sophisticated. For us it is Buddhism which broadens the community beyond our personal needs and teaches us to share resources without possessiveness. It cannot be done just by morality and good intentions, for that will pale, bore, or repress, especially the most imaginative and energetic people. A community needs a wise, wide, intentional, philosophical, and practical base that is expressed not so much by rules or philosophy itself as by the nature, details, and trivia of the daily physical activity, attitudes, and way of life.

*A community can help us become free from viewing our lives as dramas of success or failure requiring a leading actor and a series of emotional scenes*

Buddhism poses a transient world which you cannot grasp, as the Diamond Sutra states, "with past, present, or future mind." Being transient, it is suffering. The world posed is not only ecologically interdependent, but extended in all ways, in all directions, without obstruction. In this changing vast world the identity of everything is found under your own two feet. Human beings are makers. If we pick up a beachstone, we have made something. We enjoy a beachstone that someone has given us. We are always making things, and for somebody who practices meditation there is an awareness of the fullness and emptiness of

Richard Baker-roshi          49

the background out of which things are made, out of which things arise. When things are examined carefully, even in the physical terms of modern physics, they rest on the edge, the entry of arising and disappearing.

The process of meditation is to identify our self or to find our own center of balance in that space, in that emptiness that includes form and emptiness; in that activity that is the moment of expression; in that danger and security of being without support and also not needing support. The Large Sutra on Perfect Wisdom states that "a Bodhisattva who courses in perfect wisdom should survey conditioned co-production through the aspiration for space-like non-extinction." You, your aspiration, your making, is the center of existence. "Making" in this sense is another word for form itself, for the intentional identity of the phenomenal world.

What can you actually possess? How do you possess anything? I remember Suzuki-roshi taking his glasses off and saying, "These are your glasses, but you know about my tired old eyes so you let me use them." There is that kind of feeling about possession in a Buddhist community—that you cannot actually own something, that you use things through the assistance, through the kindness of others. We do not want possessions that exclude, that cause envy, that are not easily accessible to others. If you have something unusual, it is best if someone gave it to you. Everything can be understood this way, by our continuity with everything, by our inextricable oneness and place.

The second precept of Buddhism is a good example of this. It is sometimes translated as "do not steal," but actually it means "do not take what is not given." More strictly, the "do not" of all the precepts means that what you have already is enough, that you do not need anything more. Already is enough. Precepts are boundaries that only exist when they are crossed. Looking at someone you may feel a direct contact. But as soon as you wonder what kind of person or what the person is thinking, good, bad or indifferent, you have lost the contact and broken the precepts.

The first precept, "do not kill," means do not interfere with what you cannot repair or replace (including this moment). For example, it would extend to minimizing the use of non-renewable resources—try not to use so much gasoline, propane, and so

> "These are your glasses, but you know about my tired old eyes so you let me use them."

forth; try to use replaceable fuels such as wood or wind. In the Sangha this is expressed through physical activity, attitudes, and rules. When Dogen-roshi, one of the greatest Zen masters of Japan, used water from a running stream to wash his clothes, he put the water that was left over back into the stream. In a Zen monastery when you pour out waste water, you should pour it toward yourself. You will treat the water very carefully. In this way you will be aware and careful with everything, treating everything as yourself, even waste.

This physical care and expression of your situation and life are very important in Zen practice. It is a kind of field or ecological perception and proprioception. For example, although breaking a cup is a loss, it is also an opportunity for someone to sweep it up and an opportunity for someone else to mend it or to make another cup. This perception of the real as the relationships of things, rather than the isolated object, is characteristic of Buddhism and the emphasis on physical practice.

The question of what are the relationships among people that create a community which is more than just neighbors, friends, or associates would require a more extended discussion than is possible here. But at least we can say that the kind of community we are talking about is a group of people who make all major and most minor decisions communally, who share some or most of their daily activity, and who live together or in very close proximity.

The dominant bonding and controlling aspect of the Zen Center community is that we meditate together and share a daily schedule. Sharing a schedule produces the feeling of a common life, which is further reinforced by the contrast with the outside world. The schedule should also be somewhat demanding, should cause some feeling of difficulty or inconvenience. A schedule that realistically requires something from us will help a community stay together. People seldom go back twice to a movie, book, painting, or poem that makes little demand on them.

But the essence of our schedule is the zazen meditation. The deep feeling, openness, and space of zazen absorb most of the problems that would otherwise occur in a community, reducing pettiness and quarrels almost to zero. The challenge and high priority of practicing and meditating together make the problems of kitchen and grounds, of personal interactions seem relatively unimportant.

Another essential function of meditation in a community is that it is a mode for personal change in much the same way as the encounter group process works for the Synanon Foundation and Delancey Street Foundation. In a community people are always confronted with how well or poorly they function personally and with others. This would be very upsetting and would make everyone defensive if there were not a continual process of personal change and self-awareness.

The thinking, decisions, and visions of a Zen Sangha flow from the mind-of-zazen, the mind of meditation. This zazen mind is grounded in our breathing, in the physiology of heart and lungs, in concentrated attention and related thinking, expressing what the Greeks called "the unshakable truth of the well-rounded heart."

While zazen is the priority by which we relate all other aspects of the daily life, still zazen alone would not be enough. The rest of the life of the community must be a support and an extension of zazen. I have already mentioned two of the precepts, a little of the philosophy, and the importance of physical care and attention to the details of our relationships to people and things. Other examples are such important and difficult rules as not gossiping or criticizing others—rules which are often repressive or nearly impossible to follow unless you are practicing meditation. It is encouraging to find that it is possible to enjoy people and express everything we want to without gossip and the many things we often do to undermine each other. (The minute attentive practices of Abidharma psychology and mindfulness are necessary extensions of zazen too, but too much to go into in this talk.) The fundamental expression of zazen in our life is a capacity for compassionate attention to people and details.

The two most important rules of the Sangha-community are "do not hurt others" and "do not deceive others." These are especially important in guiding members of the community in love and sexual relationships. When these two common-sense rules are honestly and carefully observed, almost all of the sexual problems that beset and in fact often destroy most communities are avoided or solved. But you must be able to find the general community's good—the priority, ethics, and ethos of everyone finding a way to live together—above your own particular satisfactions. In a community it usually becomes very clear that when the price of personal satisfaction is deception and pain, it is not worth it.

These two rules will lessen the tendency of people, particularly new people, to raid the community to satisfy their pre-community fantasies and values. A community cannot survive if it is used as a source of status, sexual partners, or convenient living in a manner that is primarily meaningful in the outside world or in exclusively personal terms. There needs to be an adjustment period available for new members to find out and open themselves to the responsibilities, unique intimacy, and deep satisfactions of living in a community.

The glue or bonds of a community are different from the glue of friendship or marriage. The usual bond of marriage or friendship often will not survive time or individual personalities, and even at its best and most consistent will not sustain or hold together a community. The attempt to build a community on the basis of friendship, personality, or likes and dislikes will destroy friendships and marriages as well as founder the community. It is a mistake that has been made by numerous communes, experimental schools, growth centers, and extended living arrangements.

The actual physical space is a very important part of what makes people able to live together and develop the bonds of community. By physical space I mean also the space of sound, sight, and physical passage. The bells, drums, and sounding boards of a Buddhist community articulate and relate space and events. It is a mostly unknown environment in the West. The visual space should be varied, related, and if possible visually interlocking. The space of physical passage should be thought of according to whether people are or should be walking slowly, *Already* quickly, quietly, with care, and so forth. In Japan, temples and *is enough* other buildings of some dignity are often up a flight of outside stairs that are paced to change your pace. Level stone walkways are similarly paced and often bring you a long way around a building so that you enter it with familiarity. Most important, passage within and between buildings should be understood according to how often people will meet each other and the significance of the activities and buildings joined by the passage.

Richard Baker-roshi      53

It is best if people meet and greet each other regularly and appropriately in their passage through the day. Passage in this way can make manifest and develop the common experience of work, priorities, and associations that are the actual bonds and intentions of a community.

It is helpful if the schedule and rules work with life outside the community. The diet should not be too different from what people grew up with and what is eaten in restaurants and people's homes. How to bring up children and include non-parents, and how to maintain the nuclear family and at the same time share community life, are best developed in a way that is integrally related to the larger society. Without this, life for school age children may be especially difficult, confusing, and even disabling. In general, the way of life and schedule should permit easy access and flow between the community and the world outside the community. This should be especially true where members have outside jobs, as do the students at our San Francisco center.

Work itself, both inside and outside the community, is an essential part of practice, a way to realize the nature and needs of our environmental and social existence. Within the community we would not dream of or consider replacing a person by a machine. It is an offensive and ridiculous idea. The work we do together is too valuable to sacrifice to machines or to the saving of time. Work is our "making," the activity, the making of our being and of our material and psychological survival.

*"Zen is only two things—zazen and sweeping the temple, and it does not matter how big the temple is."*

In Buddhism the physical body is not viewed as something separate from or other or lesser than mind/spirit; and the physical world is not viewed as other than being itself, inextricably separate and joined. This is far from the physicalist view of the world as an inanimate and windable clock, far from the attempt of reductive and deterministic behaviorism to eliminate consciousness and will, and far from the attempt by many people to synthesize experience with chemicals. In Buddhism we start existentially with just what is in front of us and is effective now. Life continues from this spot and is complete on this spot. Life is not a picture in front of you, a destiny, not something you can synthesize. The aspects of your present situation are actually you and your path. ("Mind only" or "material only" comes to the same, if we actually try impossibly to "account for," to take everything into account. Cybernetics and Buddhist logic can come together here.)

It is from this premise that we started the Neighborhood Foundation—start sweeping the streets in front of the building. Start somewhere immediately. Right in front of you. The poet and Zen teacher Gary Snyder's own Zen teacher, shortly before he died, told Gary that "Zen is only two things—zazen and sweeping the temple, and it does not matter how big the temple is." The Neighborhood Foundation is part of the permeable membrane of the Zen Center community and now includes a neighborhood track team, a low rent program, special assistance to many neighborhood groups and individuals, neighborhood and park maintenance, a local community garden, tree planting, recycling, food distribution, and many other things—all begun from starting to sweep the street.

The various ways we are becoming self-supporting also started as extensions of what we were already doing. Right Livelihood is the fifth step of what is called the Eightfold Path in Buddhism. The eight are Right Views, Right Thought, Right Speech, Right Conduct, Right Livelihood, Right Effort, Right Mindfulness, and Right Concentration. Right Livelihood means that whatever you do should not in any way harm or deceive people. Suzuki-roshi insisted that we protect other people's livelihood before we think of our own. For a number of years he would not let us start a bookstore. He said, with a force critical of our thoughtlessness, that we should support the local bookstores. It was not until we had a library that he allowed us to start a bookstore as part of the library.

*Life is not a picture in front of you, a destiny, not something you can synthesize. The aspects of your present situation are actually you and your path*

In a similar way we should be careful not to use our advantages as a community with extended connections and inexpensive labor costs in a way that hurts the competitors of the Tassajara Bread Bakery and the Green Gulch Greengrocer. Rather than lowering prices too much, we should offer more service and better products made with better ingredients. The emphasis in a Buddhist community is on cooperative and not competitive interdependence. Competitiveness is usually motivated by an attempt to create some static safe unchanging situation. Actual interdependence is more dangerous than that. We can take pleasure in other people's success.

A Sangha-community is organized and defined in a way that does not produce winners and losers. We are not always trying to turn verbs into nouns, process into gains, learning into education (a tendency Ivan Illich has pointed out). In a Sangha, status is not determined by skill, talent, or winning. Status is determined primarily by seniority, commitment, kindness, flexibility, receptivity and similar attitudes. Authority and decision-making are based on consensus through seniority—for example, members of five years have roughly the same participation and authority. Positions are rotated, giving everyone a chance to develop. It means that you may be head cook at some point, even though you do not know how to cook, and that you can expect people to support you in doing the best you can.

*Leadership by talent alone develops leaders and followers but not leaders who develop*

Without this approach the most talented people, or those with the most desire or need to excel, or those with developed social skills, will take over the community and decision-making very rapidly. When talent or winning is the premium, a fairly new member with great talent, but without experience or wisdom, can take over a community that is not articulated through consensus and seniority. Leadership by talent alone develops leaders and followers but not leaders who develop. When development of all the members of the community is emphasized, then the wisdom of the community can flow through everyone. Community can awaken our capacity to know and experience the reaches and great satisfactions of our mental and physical life, of our individual and extended life.

In this talk I have tried to touch on many aspects of community that may be useful to anyone and any community. Our society needs every kind of community, every meaning of the word community, if it is to survive. Laws and wealth alone cannot hold us together.

In America the identity and good of the individual has been given such singular priority that everything else, every association, all agencies, the government, the land, even the environment and the planet are seen as serving the individual, his or her property and opportunities. (On the other side in the Orient the emphasis is too much on everything serving the community.) Much of our urban and rural population sees the government, business, and the church as personal sources of welfare payments, employment, and charity. Few people understand or act through the responsibility and originality of association and mutuality.

We have made opportunities for free enterprise and individual liberties; now we need to make opportunities for the enterprises and identities of community to develop new liberties and new individual identities. We fear this idea, but there is no alternative. Laws are meant to arbitrate; you cannot legislate the common good, that is the province of community, of living together with kindness and practicality.

*Our society needs every kind of community, every meaning of the word community, if it is to survive*

Community is that compassionate good will and realistic regard for others, for ourselves, that makes laws mostly unnecessary to enforce the common weal, the common good. Without this regard, as it arises and is developed by community, our society will not establish or maintain humane order—a social order that is the natural expression and necessary basis of individual freedom.

Richard Baker-roshi       57

Elise Boulding is Director of the Institute for Behavioral Science and Professor of Sociology at the University of Colorado in Boulder. She is the translator of Fred Polak's The Image of the Future, *the author of* The Underside of History *and a member of* The Institute for World Order.

# 5 Women in Community

## Elise Boulding

It's a little ironic for me to be given the assignment of talking about community, because this is my year of solitude. I'm on leave from the university, and I'm living in a hermitage in the mountains. I'm living in total aloneness, or all-oneness as Brother David called it yesterday, and total silence. (I do see my family once a week.) And in some ways I have very different perceptions of community now as a result of that experience of solitude.

If you live in silence, you discover, as do those of you who get up early in the morning before people get up, that there are lots of sounds in silence. The sounds which aren't humanly generated give you a very different feeling for reality than sounds that are humanly generated. The companionship that comes out of solitude is very different from the companionship that comes out of human relatedness. For each person who lives in solitude, that companionship will take on the characteristics of what that person can receive, but I suppose one way I would describe it would be as a kind of a God-saturatedness. And so, perhaps, the theme, which I understand has been the continual dialectic during the conference, of contemplation versus activism is very relevant for me to speak to.

I have found by my withdrawal a sense of connectedness with the planetary society that I never had before, a commitment to action in a different sense, perhaps, than I understood action before, and a kind of resolution of the need for attention to inner space and the attention outward, the need for society.

In a way, this isn't something that just happened recently. My earliest childhood memories certainly are of this moving back and forth between experiencing God's presence and doing things such as visiting old people's homes at Christmas and Easter, and, as I got into the teen years, doing surveys of housing in the slum areas of the town where I lived. Then gradually I moved into the householder's role and the whole range of community activism, always weaving back and forth between times of prayer and profound experiences of God's presence—and with a sense, always, that this had to be translated. The process of translation has been the continual theme; the peaks and the troughs which Brother David spoke of so illuminatingly yesterday were a part of that pattern of life.

But in one of those periods that come to all of us, and which came to me when I was fifty-one, I got ripped apart, you might say, from head to foot. And all of the kinds of syntheses and integrations and weaving in and out of a prayer life and the activist life were not working any more. Perhaps part of the problem was that I lost the sense of boundary between myself and society; every problem was my problem, every problem demanded my attention. There was no point at which to say, "Yes, this. No, not that." And so this total involvement gradually became clear; I had a total lack of discernment. I suppose this lack of boundaries, this need to rediscover discernment, set the stage for my year of withdrawal. I know all resolutions are provisional in this life, but for the time being I feel that I have a new perception of the importance of discernment and of time spent in the act of discernment.

Before moving directly to a discussion of communities in relation to this, I'd like to say something about the relation of psychic phenomena to the problems of social change and to religious development. We had yesterday a very moving account of this realm of human experience and its relevance for community life. The value of the psychic realm in religious experience and in increasing one's capacity to deal with the environment was pointed out last night; you get a much more multi-dimensional understanding. David Spangler gave a beautiful and delightfully humorous presentation about the plants teaching the people in the Findhorn community, about the forty pound cabbages, and about the money that turns up through manifestation when you've started a building. It reminded me very much of the evangelical fundamentalist environment I was in as a child in the Ocean Grove community; men and women would stand up and testify to these miraculous things that had happened to their businesses through prayer. We smile at these stories but they also have some kind of validity. When you have been touched by them, they affect how you respond to life. There is an expansion of awareness that goes through this and it should not be denied. The kind of teaching that our environment does for us is my daily experience in my own hermitage. So I'm personally grateful that these things were brought in here. They are precious and it's certainly time that we introduced them as a part of human formation.

But David also spoke of the limitations of the psychic realm. There is perhaps the problem of the fallacy of misplaced concreteness because of undue attention to this area without any perception of its limitations. The limitations of psychic phenomena are that they do not deal with the problem of discernment; and there is still the need to discern, the need to analyze, the need to make judgments and the need to find applications.

This problem of teaching discernment and developing discernment in communities is, I think, one of the most challenging tasks that face us. Religious communities, or communities with some religious orientation, have not always done well with children. In fact, I have observed many people in the years since my own adulthood, adults of my own age and younger, who were products of the previous generation of communities and had been damaged

Elise Boulding    61

in various ways. I see the problem of human formation as much more complex than do most communitarians. Just as the experimental and open-minded teacher in the classroom simplifies in one way, the experimental and open-minded person in the community simplifies the product, the child, in another way. Maybe you have to be fifty-four to have seen enough children growing up and what they're able to do as adults to realize the depth of the problem, how difficult it is to help human beings become whole and function as whole persons through an adult life.

So, I'll discuss communities (and not just the Lindisfarne type, but try to put it in the context of all the different kinds of communities we have) in terms of two things, the human formation, the creation of a new kind of a human product, and the creation of working models for the future of the sociosphere. I think those are the twin concerns that most communities address themselves to.

I do not share the general optimism about this being a great time for the creation of the new planetary community. I did share that optimism up until about a year ago, when I started becoming more and more aware of what I consider the special handicaps we have in the twentieth century in terms of facing that creation. We certainly are standing at thresholds. If we speak in terms of axial periods in human history, this is the threshold. Nobody's going to deny that. But we have certain handicaps that perhaps did not exist in the past.

One is the thinness of the mankind concept. It's thin for a variety of reasons. Both Saul Mendlovitz and Dick Falk spoke about the fact that we are a very privileged majority/minority here; we're a majority in our use of the world's resources and so on. When people first began talking about planetary community—from 1850 to 1900 was the first modern statement—they had no conception of the blacks or the third world. All that has now entered consciousness. So when we now say "mankind," we at least know that it comes in different colors and that it speaks different languages, which people didn't know in 1900—they didn't know it in that sense of knowing it with their full, conscious, attentive minds, although in some rational corner they obviously knew that people were of different kinds.

But what we still do not know in that sense relates very much to the use of the words "man" and "mankind." And the language which has been used here this week, "planetary man," the future of "man" and "mankind," has to do with a kind of a crippling of our capacity to conceptualize the nature of the human being and the human condition because of our linguistic practices. The generic use of the word "man" simply cripples our minds, and I'm not just making a political statement, although it has definite political implications. In the Sociological Association, we have spent a lot of time trying to teach our male colleagues to understand what the use of the word "man" in sociology has done to distort sociology. And I'm saying that exactly that kind of thing happens among futurists and among people who are concerned with spiritual dimensions and development; this is the worst place for it to remain so firmly entrenched. So, I invite you to remove the words "man" and "mankind" from your vocabulary and to struggle with using the alternatives. Maybe some-day we can use "man" and it won't matter, but not in this century, friends—so, "human," the "human being," the "human person," "humankind." There's another approach that helps us uncripple our minds, and it has to do with thinking in terms of the sisterhood of humankind instead of the brotherhood, or the Motherhood of God instead of the Fatherhood. The church has been severely crippled for two thousand years, the Christian Church, by the entirely male concepts of Divinity. That's why I say we arrive crippled at the point of creating the new person, the new era, the new stage in social evolution. We just may not be the ones to do it, because we have all these fatherhood and brotherhood concepts.

*The generic use of the word "man" simply cripples our minds*

Now, all community formation has to do, among other things, with problems of scale. The population of the planet has been steadily increasing for a long time, so periodically we arrive at new critical densities. Just where you say a critical breaking point is depends on how you want to cut up history, but we do recognize that we arrive at new points of critical density; then we have problems of scale. How do you organize society, given these new densities? How do you redistribute resources? This was not a problem in hunting and gathering societies; it was not a problem in the earliest subsistence agriculture. But after these stages this problem of social organization and redistribution arose. There were problems of social bonding which didn't exist before in a familistic or a totally enclosed village life. There was now the problem of how to relate to people. What are the skills and methods and alliance mechanisms in everything from friendship (when friends aren't simply the people that grew up together) to marriage and the formation of special purpose organizations? (Of course the religious societies were the first special purpose organizations.) So, every community deals with these issues, new forms of social organization, new ways of social bonding and new ways of developing human beings.

Now let's look at the history of communities. Taking the period roughly from 50,000 to 2,000 B.C., the first communities were, in fact, literally sisterhoods, sibylline communities, sibylline priestesshoods — all of the earliest experiences of community formation, that is, outside the family, were by women. By 500 B.C. a new point of critical density had been passed. The Jainists and the Buddhists and a whole proliferation of religious orders that were communities grew. They had to deal with problems of scale because there was already runaway urbanization in 500 B.C. So all the problems of bondedness and of redistribution of resources that were being held by powerful military elites had to be faced. Most of these communities were elitist; some were esoteric. The sibylline sisterhoods continued, there were Pythagorean communities, and so on.

The Christian era introduced a new kind of community, because the earliest Christian communities had both women and men and were not esoteric. There was an initiation rite, because there was baptism, but the unusual quality of these communities was that they were for working people, not just for the elite. And they followed the trade routes. One of the strengths of early Christianity was its women traders; they cut their hair and dressed as men, and they travelled. When women are actively involved in international trade, a whole set of bonding capacities and of spiritual potentialities exist side by side. So the rapid spread of Christianity had to do with the role of women traders. The apostles, women like Secla, very dynamic people of deep, powerful spiritual awareness with a gift of teaching and of creating communities, went from one place to another helping set up new Christian communities. There were many women like her, working side by side with men. On the one hand were the apostles, both women and men apostles; on the other hand were

*All of the earliest experiences of community formation, outside the family, were by women*

the traders, who were friends of the apostles, and threw open their houses in all the towns where they had trading centers. This allowed a very interesting interaction that drew in the scholars of the time, creating a crosscutting or intersecting of the scholarly and scientific community, the trade community and the religious community. The explosion of Christianity around 100 A.D. was a function of the interaction of the three and of the important role of women in all three of them.

Now in the 1200's, again there was a new set of social densities because of a fantastic population explosion, and so again there was the need to find new ways of bonding, new ways of redistributing the resources. (I'm speaking especially of Europe now.) Almost every kind of community that's been founded in the last hundred years was also founded in the 1200's and 1300's—fantastic proliferation of every conceivable kind. And in the Middle Ages again, women were very much involved. There were great women religious teachers like Julian of Norwich. Twenty-five percent of the landed estates of Europe were administered by women in the 1200's because of the evacuation migrations related to the crusades. Women were very active at the heart of the trade network and at the heart of each major sector of life. So, again all these things were interrelating and intersecting, providing a terrific capability; the post-bureaucratic age was almost entered in the 1300's, the Joachim de Fiorie Age of the Holy Spirit with the dismantling of all bureaucratic structures. But we didn't make it; we slid back.

Many parallels can be drawn between that period and our own. But the one thing we don't have now, as I pointed out before, is the involvement of women. We don't have women in the trade networks of the world, and we have very few religious women of stature that we can really draw on as spiritual resources of the planet. They're there, but they're not in a position where they're audible and visible. So we enter this era, where we have many other enabling mechanisms, many other new understandings, crippled in that respect, and also crippled in the sense that most of our social innovations still derive pretty much from the 1200's and 1300's. I think Francis figured out a lot of things to do with large scale populations and redistribution that we have not particularly improved on. The decentralist theory of today isn't that much of an advance. So we still have a lot of work to do.

*Almost every kind of community that's been founded in the last hundred years was also founded in the 1200's and 1300's*

Elise Boulding 65

Then what have we, in fact, been creating in the way of communities that will develop new forms of organization suitable for transition to a future planetary society and will develop the kind of people who can function in it? How are our communities dealing with new ways of human formation, new forms of bonding people who otherwise would have difficulty finding places in the social organization? Almost every type of community that we have today has a residential base. Lindisfarne, in a way, is a residential community; you have a core here. At the other end are all the people who like to come to Lindisfarne, and all the other associations that are supportive of communities. So each type of community has a residential core and then various voluntary associations that support it and act on behalf of it, with people moving back and forth. The residential commitment uses the oldest model we have of human bonding, which is the family, deriving its strength from some familistic commitments. The people who support that structure and move in and out of it are providing the other ingredient which the human being has had as a part of his life in our entire history on the planet—fluidity, migration and movement. One thing we have done very well in the twentieth century is to find ways to have centers. We know where they are and we know how to find them and we know how to move in and out of them. Sometimes we're insecure about how central we are, how much we belong, what our identity is. I think our challenge lies precisely in this fluidity. And that, as I understand it, is what this new community that David is working with in California is trying to do, using the troubadour principle.

The contemplatives and the apostolics are today very much at the forefront of the creation of an understanding of new modes of living. The troubadour principle, interestingly enough, is the one that's being considered by all the women apostolic orders that I'm familiar with; they are organizing themselves into small fluid groups that can move around. Yet they have a commitment to a very deeply centered prayer life, and they are at one and the same time studying new methods of spiritual formation and new methods of moving about in community. They are also very much committed to organizing the empowerment of local community. In local empowerment, they're helping people figure out how to use what they have in their local community, instead of dealing with bureaucratic structures of the church or of the government. So

there is an enormous resource there which goes far beyond anything that we're aware of; they're helping build new localist type
infrastructures. The contemplatives, at the same time that the
apostolics are studying spiritual formation, are taking the action
dimension of how far prayer reaches. Brother David is one of the
best examples I know of a contemplative relating to the world of
action, so I don't need to say anything more about that.

The complex of communities that Lindisfarne represents and
that the community in Scotland and the other new consciousness
communities represent takes human formation, the formation of
the new person, as almost the central point. And one of the
things that I'm most interested in is seeing how there can be
more interaction between those and the political communities like
the Movement for a New Society, where you have people coming
together out of the same depth of commitment to the New World.
People who enter the Movement for a New Society, just as people
entering religious orders, leave behind private property—in
effect, they take a vow of poverty. Their vow of obedience is an
interesting one because it's obedience to the political needs of
society, a rather different concept of obedience than the one
we're used to. So they're committing their total lives in an almost
monastic way to a new discovery of the political potentialities of
the twentieth century. In the places where I have seen them at
work, in Denver, in Philadelphia and at a new one in the Rocky
Mountains of Colorado, they are reading maps and creating new
kinds of maps on the social terrain. They come into a community
and create a map, put things on a map that nobody knew were
there—the resources, people who can help each other. Then they
teach the community, while they themselves are learning, what
these resources are—the old self-sufficiency thing. But it has a
new meaning because it's done with a very heightened political
consciousness and a sense of a knowledge of what's happening in
Europe, what's happening in Africa, what's happening in Asia.
There is active communication and a full use of the mechanism of
travel. So there really is a creation of a new political
infrastructure which has network capabilities. You have people
like Tony Judge sitting in Brussels designing a computer
information system that you and I can use to communicate with
whomever we want to anywhere. Now this is localism using the
most highly developed technology. But these New Society

communities are also familistic, with a very intimate daily life and responsibility for human formation; they're raising children. The residents are of all ages, but they all worry about their lack of time for inner growth. If you could just perform an operation and link together a Lindisfarne and a Life Center of the Movement for a New Society, then you would be relating all these very skilled political infrastructure things with these very new and insightful understandings about inner growth. It's a challenge; I think it's one of the things we really have to relate to.

The New Town movement should not be ignored as we think about communities. A lot of people are putting their energies into New Towns and they do represent an interesting intermediate level. Having participated in the formation of a New Town in Colorado, I'm intimately aware of the possibilities for sticking in a whole new political conception of local development and of bringing together, at the very start, people of all kinds of different socioeconomic and ethnic backgrounds. New Towns try to create and design spaces for the formation of the spirit as well as to amplify people's social skills. They try to keep a spiritual dimension. The kind of alliance you get when you're building a New Town is fantastic—local business magnates and their bankers, people from the churches, commune and counter-culture people, and all the ethnic minorities (if you are skillful in making your contacts). Women are given a very fine opportunity to do a lot of community design work. The communities that have actually developed have all fallen so far short of this vision of a new system of alliances in contemporary society that it's tragic. But the possibilities are still there.

The one kind of community that didn't exist in the 1200's (there were lots of New Towns in the Middle Ages) is the Gay Liberation commune. This particular phenomenon is new to our time. I think it's a transition phenomenon, but it is a very significant mobilization of human potentials that crosscuts the religious and political in a very interesting way. I don't know how to put that into the broader picture except to say that it's a transition type of community, but a very, very important one.

For every one of the communities I've talked about, there are counterparts, network counterparts, people not living in the community but working in the networks that link the communities. Networking is where it's at for the twentieth century. So how do we take advantage of our networking capacities and our new understandings of the possibilities of fluidity and relationship to centers and still find enough time to work on that problem of human formation? I came here because I see this as the problem that keeps eluding us. We get everything else set up—we set up all these potentials—and then we lose the whole thing because we haven't dealt adequately with formation. But formation cannot be separated from the problem of social structure. In the formation process there must be a linking to a continued training in sharp analytic work—to get fuzzy minded because you feel spiritual is one of the greatest dangers. Touchy-feely spirituality is another very great danger.

I think I've begun to understand a way of linking the training of the intuitive capacity with the training of the analytic capacity that I'm hoping to explore further in a teaching situation. It has to do with taking any phenomenon (I started this in teaching about ecosystems) and having students conceptualize, choose one ecosystem. They chose things like the rooms they lived in on campus, or the State Legislature. Then they had to conceptualize that in a series of different modes. First they did it verbal-analytic.(Our entire education is linked to verbal-analytic conceptualizations; our examinations are couched in those terms. So everybody, through his entire school career, has to reduce everything there is in reality to verbal-analytic.) After the verbal-analytic they were asked to transform it into metaphor, the same ecosystem in a metaphor. Third assignment, turn it into color; fourth assignment, turn it into music; fifth assignment, turn it into a mathematical equation; next, turn it into poetry. By the time each person had conceptualized his ecosystem in each of these different modes, all kinds of perceptions had been generated, and understandings of the multi-dimensionality of phenomena. I could have lectured until I was blue in the face and they would not have understood in that way.

I think you come closer in places like Lindisfarne than anywhere else to making these perceptions a whole. It would be a fantastic contribution for communities to make this a part of the formation process for children growing up, so that they wouldn't go through this destroying process of rendering everything into the verbal-analytic mode. Along with this linking of the intuitive and the analytic, communities could also teach the skills of familism. Many church parishes are developing extended family programs now. For example, twenty people sign up and are put together in a family. Then for a year they spend a day together every week. These groups don't work unless they have a nuclear family or two in them. Unless a couple of the people have all the disciplines of a family formed by a sustained family relationship, the groups can't continue the bonding. They simply break apart before the program year is over. So there are certain kinds of mutual accommodation, mutual self-discipline, and so on, that people learn in families, which we shouldn't despise. We say a lot about how the family is breaking up, but it's an empirical fact that certain kinds of skills develop in nuclear families that very much need to be introduced into communities.

*Certain kinds of skills develop in nuclear families that very much need to be introduced into communities*

So the linking of the intellectual-analytic and the spiritual-intuitive through one set of devices, and the introduction of the skills of familistic bonding into a context of being full of the love of God and glorifying His creation, while being a part of its evolution, is possible in our century. It may not be probable, but it's possible.

---

*Paolo Soleri was born in Italy and received his Ph.D. in architecture from the Turin Polytechnic Institute. He came to the U.S. in 1947 to study with Frank Lloyd Wright at Taliesin West. The author of* Arcology: The City in the Image of Man *and* Matter Becoming Spirit, *he is the founder and director of the Cosanti Foundation. Currently he is directing the construction of Arcosanti.*

# 6 The City of the Future

## Paolo Soleri

The problem I am confronting is the present design of cities only a few stories high, stretching outward in unwieldy sprawl for miles. As a result of their sprawl, they literally transform the earth, turn farms into parking lots and waste enormous amounts of time and energy transporting people, goods and services over their expanses. My solution is urban implosion rather than explosion. In nature, as an organism evolves it increases in complexity, and it also becomes a more compact or miniaturized system. The city too is an organism, one that should be as alive and functional as any living creature. It must follow the same process of complexification and miniaturization to become a more lively container for the social, cultural and spiritual evolution of man.

The central concept around which these developments revolve is that of Arcology—architecture and ecology as one integral process. Arcology is capable, at least theoretically, of demonstrating positive responses to the many problems of urban man, those of population, pollution, energy and natural resource depletion, food scarcity and quality of life. Arcology is the methodology that recognizes the necessity of the radical reorganization of the sprawling urban landscape into dense, integrated, three-dimensional cities. The city structure must contract, or miniaturize, in order to support the complex activities that sustain cultural man and give him new perception and renewed trust in society and its future. A central tenet of Arcology is that the city is the necessary instrument for the evolution of man.

I see the idea of Arcology, particularly Arcosanti (the prototype now under construction near Cordes Junction, Arizona), as a step beyond the present city. Arcosanti will house a great number of people per acre compared with today's two-dimensional cities, and the surrounding land will be left for agriculture, recreation and natural wildlife. Arcosanti is designed so that its residents will live in the outer surfaces, their habitats open to light and air, facing out to nature and also in to the city. Both the lively heart of the city, on the one hand, with its parks, commercial areas, schools, theaters and public spaces, and the natural surroundings, on the other hand, will be but a few minutes away by foot, bicycle, elevator or pedestrian transport system.

*A central tenet of Arcology is that the city is the necessary instrument for the evolution of man*

An important focus of the design development of Arcologies, especially in terms of Arcosanti, is energy efficiency. My recent work investigates the potentials of solar effects in a series of Arcology designs, the intent being the development of a central system for the efficient collection, transmission and consumption of the solar energy needed to support the population of a town or city. Recent research is directed toward the use of large-scale, terraced greenhouses, sloping toward the south, which act as solar heat collectors. The result of such greenhouses will be not only local intensive food production, but also an energy support system which will use redirected solar heat to meet the basic hot water, space heating and cooling needs of the town.

The thesis is simple: there are a few physical and biological phenomena, which I call effects, known, used or lived by man which by intent and by design can be brought together in such a way as to act upon one another "in pursuit" of a synthesis useful to mankind. All of these effects have been a part of the human scene for about as long as man has been part of the living world. The four inorganic effects, the Greenhouse Effect, the Chimney Effect, the Apse Effect and the Heat Sink Effect are consequences of physical laws. The two organic effects characterize themselves differently. The Horticulture Effect, as a latecomer, is a conscious intervention of man in organic processes. The Urban Effect has its origin with the origin of life itself, 4,000 million years or so before man enters the moving stage of evolution.

The Greenhouse Effect enables the collection of warmth from the sun inside a defined space. When combined with the Horticultural Effect this provides a natural agricultural base.

The Chimney Effect is the system by which the collected warm air may be channelled as it rises.

The Apse Effect is the capacity of certain structures, similar to acoustic shells open to the south, to be sun collectors when the sun is low on the horizon (winter) and sun shades when the sun is high on the horizon (summer).

The Heat Sink Effect is the use of the capacity of mass (stone, concrete, water, etc.) to store heat when the surrounding temperature is higher than its own and to give it back when the surrounding temperature is lower than its own.

The Horticultural Effect has its origin in the early times when man began to control the growth of selected kinds of greenery.

The Urban Effect antedates by eons such effects. It is fundamentally that phenomenon in which two or more particles of physical matter begin to interact in ways other than statistical and fatal (Laws of Physics)—that is to say, the ways which are organic or living and, eventually, the instinctive, conscious, self-conscious, mental, cultural, spiritual ways. The methodology underlying such escalation is the methodology of complexity and miniaturization, that is to say, the more and more stringent synthesis of means and ends, of media becoming messages, of ultimate economy and frugality. It is the Urban Effect that is the magnet around which the whole living experiment is clustering itself in search of that potentially ultimate manifestation man has often called God.

Paolo Soleri    75

Around this magnet is also designed the concept of the Two Suns Arcology. Arcology: the ecological nature of the architecture of the urban system. Two Suns: one, the physical sun, the source of all life on the planet; the other, the offspring sun of the first, expressed in the monumental miracle of evolution peaked by the spirit of man.

In the Two Suns Arcology, then, there is an attempt to define physical and metaphysical conditions that will see the interactive (cybernetic) co-presence of the Greenhouse Effect, the Chimney Effect, the Apse Effect, the Heat Sink Effect, the Horticultural Effect and the Urban Effect to the end of defining a living system coherent with the physical, organic and spiritual facets of the dynamic system we call reality.

The central figures of the program are man and the sun. Since the technologies and the hardware for implementation are elementary, the concept can have universal application throughout the climate belt of the earth endowed with sunshine. At least two thirds of humankind is living in such a belt, which goes to cover a variety of conditions from the coastal areas to the mountain landscapes. Of this belt, optimum areas would be those with small rainfall, the arid zones, for five main reasons: 1) high percentage of sunny days, 2) the necessity of careful water management, 3) the high desirability of contained, dense urban systems, 4) the desirability of foodstuff produced locally for local consumption at a minimal water use, 5) the effectiveness of evaporative cooling in dry climates.

*The energy crisis is a crisis of the spirit*

The concept is then in scale with the global problem of energy, which is only the tip of the iceberg. The iceberg is made up of natural resources scarcity, food scarcity, space scarcity and spiritual scarcity. It just happens that these same scarcities are "focused" upon by the Two Suns Arcology, since the arcological system is the methodology which by intent is at the point of convergence of all these problems "on the verge of resolution."

In summary, the energy crisis is a crisis of the spirit. But the spirit is the offspring of the mass-energy universe. Therefore, a crisis of the spirit is necessarily tied to a dysfunction of the "material world." We are the victims of our own materialism because such materialism has failed to understand that its own entelechy ought to be the transfiguration of the physical world into the metaphysics of consciousness, knowledge and creation. The mandatory gate to the universe of consciousness, knowledge and creation is the gate of complexity-miniaturization. The complex miniaturized is the frugal. It does more with less. The city of the two suns, the sun father of mass-energy and the sun son of the spirit, is the complex miniaturized city which is at the same time capable of plugging itself directly into the energy tide of the sun father and "consuming" such energy into spirit. The combined effects of the Greenhouse, the Chimney, the Apse, the Heat Sink, the Horticultural, and the Urban Effects compose a springboard for a synthesis which might bring forth the unexpected and the new—the future, an ever-so-slight advance toward the synthesis of the Omega God.

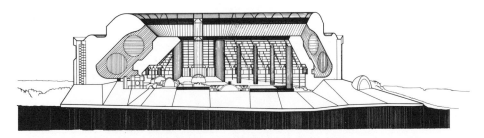

**Arcosanti, a Two Suns Arcology.**
**Drawing of South elevation and photograph of area currently under construction.**

Paolo Soleri    77

Sean Wellesley-Miller was born in England and received his B.S.C. and M.S in architecture at the London School of Economics. He has taught at the University of Delft and at MIT and was involved with "Event Structures" in Amsterdam. He is currently a partner in Suntek Research Associates of Corte Madera, California, a firm that designs and produces solar energy systems.

# Towards a Symbiotic Architecture

# 7

## *Sean Wellesley-Miller*

Let me begin by laying down some facts in a brick-by-brick fashion. As you will see, these facts pile up quite quickly and almost seem to wall industrial society into a corner. But these brick-like facts can also become steps by which we climb up to get a better perspective on our man-made world.

Nearly all "modern" phenomena can be characterized as being on the exponential slope of an S-shaped growth curve. The built environment is no exception.

World wide, more buildings will have to be built during the next fifty years than have been built throughout human history.

Even in the U.S.A., with stable population growth, the equivalent of a town of about 400,000 inhabitants is constructed once every eight weeks. (This indicates that the demand for hospitals, community centers, shopping malls, etc., is more a function of real income than of population growth **per se,** i.e., the built environment will continue to expand even if global population is stabilized.)

The built environment is the most extensive physical interface, after agriculture, between us and the natural environment.

Over relatively large parts of the Earth's land mass the built environment is becoming co-extensive with the natural environment.

Once the built environment exceeds a certain density and extent, it becomes an operating part of the Earth's biosphere, entering atmospheric, biological and hydrological cycles and altering climate, flora and fauna and the structure of regional ecologies, often irreversibly.

Buildings, individually and collectively, form the phenomenological envelope within which we spend our lives. Everyday reality is a built reality. In Western technological society 85 percent of the population spend 90 percent of their lives in man-made urban and suburban environments, 80 percent of it in buildings.

The way the built environment looks and functions conditions our idea of the way the world works. Architecture makes man as much as man makes architecture; this circularity can be a cause of distortion as well as continuity. For example, it is difficult to relate the water that comes out of the tap with the watershed area needed to collect it, the food we cook in our kitchen with the land area needed to grow it, the energy we use to light and heat our homes with the mines and oil fields needed to provide it, the wood and paper we use with the forests that provide the fiber, and so on. Our architecture has, in experiential terms, been disconnected from its support base.

Buildings are the longest-lived artifacts we make. The average life of a building is about sixty years, or about the same as the life spans of the individuals and organizations that inhabit it.

The annual output of the U.S. building industry is equal to 2.3 percent of the existing building stock. At the rate of about two million building starts a year, it would theoretically take about fifty years, and probably more like a century, to replace all buildings currently existing, assuming that this is either possible or desirable.

The median age-date of today's building stock is 1957. The median age-date of the building stock in 1990 will probably be 1977. A building constructed today will last well into the next millenium. In making these buildings, we make the mold within which much of the future will have to fit and function. While this can be a source of stability in an age of exponential change, it can also become a crippling liability in a world of limited and insufficient resources.

There is a high probability that recoverable resources of oil, gas, uranium and other primary raw materials such as chrome and copper will be exhausted within the life span of buildings made today.

It is almost a tautology to say that architecture is a response to demographic structure and distribution. U.S. population growth has doubled every forty-five years, less than a life span. The building stock has grown with it.

The principal features of current U.S. demography are the relative predominance of the immediate postwar age group and the advent of near zero population growth.

Consequently, the life history of this age group is likely to determine the social history of America. For instance, gerontology is likely to be a big industry by the next century when retired people will outnumber the work force. The postwar generation has already had major impacts on music, clothing, educational systems, sexual mores, politics and our life styles in general. Now in their late twenties and early thirties, this same age group is entering the housing market.

If maintained, the near zero population growth of the U.S. implies that the **residential** building stock may not need to grow as fast in the future as it has in the past. Renovating and retro-fitting existing buildings will become a major architectural activity. Similarly, any changes in the way buildings function will have to be applicable to existing buildings to have any impact on a national scale.

Homes are the end-locale of most consumption and the generation point of most demand. Consumption in residential and commercial buildings accounts for 22 percent of the nation's energy budget. Another 20 percent is consumed commuting between them. Home consumption accounts for 70 percent of all foodstuffs; 75 percent of all packaging materials ends up in homes.

A modern home is a habitat connected to the technostructure by at least two wires, three pipes and a road—electricity and telephone, gas, water and sewage and a car.

Food, water, energy and shelter are basic necessities. Since the beginning of the industrial revolution we have moved increasingly from a socially-evolved to a contractor-developed to a centrally-planned environment; from a material-building vocabulary based on local materials—timber, brick and adobe—to one based on industrial materials—steel, concrete, glass, aluminum and plastics; from buildings made by tools to buildings made by machines; from wood and coal-heated buildings to oil, gas and, now, electrically heated buildings. The ''technologization'' of architecture has made it subject to the same problems that haunt Western technological society as a whole. To the extent that the built environment has become dependent on the functioning of centralized technological infrastructure, it has become less viable as part of our basic life-support structures.

The majority of the existing U.S. building stock was constructed on the assumption of continuing low energy costs. As a result, the ''energy crisis'' made 60 percent of the U.S. building stock technically obsolete overnight. (This same stricture applies to U.S. production machinery, transport systems and industrialized architecture.)

One BTU in twelve of world energy production is used to heat and cool the U.S. building stock.

On average it takes as much energy to heat and cool the U.S. building stock for three years as it took to build it in the first place. Home furnaces are the largest source of air pollution after automobiles, dumping an estimated 8.4 million tons of air-pollutants into the atmosphere each year.

The materials currently employed in modern American architecture—steel, concrete, glass, plastics, aluminum and asphalt—are all among the most energy intensive materials there are.

More money is invested in the nation's building stock of sixty-seven million residential units and twenty-eight million commercial buildings than in anything else.

The purchase of a house is the largest single investment most people make in their lifetimes. The average price of a single family residence has jumped from four-to-six times annual average income to ten times annual average income.

In many parts of the U.S., domestic utility bills, i.e., the operating costs of a home, currently exceed mortgage payments.

Approximately one third of the nation's collected water supply is piped to houses and commercial buildings.

All water used in buildings, no matter for what purpose, exits as sewage.

Our water and sewage systems are coupled in series. We quite literally defecate in our water systems in the name of personal hygiene.

From a biological viewpoint water supplies are being polluted by all segments of industrial society—by agriculture through eutrophication by fertilizers and by industry through chemical wastes.

An average house uses between 150 and 200 gallons of water per inhabitant per day. The building stock as a whole uses an estimated forty billion gallons of water per year. Water usage for all purposes, agricultural, domestic and industrial, is rising rapidly; supplies are limited.

The average home produces 4.5 pounds of garbage per person per day, or anywhere from 2.5 to 5 tons per year.

Fibers, plastics, paper, wood, glass, metal and food scraps are usually all thrown in the same trash can. A lot of highly organized material input channels are combined into one "noisy" exit channel and dumped; disorder or entropy is maximized. Subsequent sorting costs make recycling uneconomic in many cases.

Homes pollute flows of materials as thoroughly as they infect water systems. Mixing organic and inorganic wastes makes frequent trash collection a necessity if disease vectors imported by waste food putrefaction are to be avoided. The necessity for frequent collection of small amounts of mixed materials again makes recycling prohibitively expensive.

The BTU value of garbage thrown out by a family of four over a year in the Boston area is equal to between a quarter and a third of the winter heating requirements of a conventional house.

In constructing this rather daunting but far from exhaustive list, I have tried to maintain a macro-operational viewpoint. Although all these statements can be viewed as simple facts

Sean Wellesley-Miller    83

about our built environment considered as a whole, they can also be viewed as a rather unsystematic collection of "system statements" about architectural energy and material flows, growth rates and contextual parameters. They are, in short, statements about the way contemporary architecture as a whole interacts with the natural environment on the one hand and the industrial and commercial sectors of our society on the other.

The macro-model of architecture that emerges is admittedly disturbing, but the analysis should not be dismissed as yet another "doom prognosis" in the face of which we are helpless as individuals. Of all major industries, architecture is distinguished as being a context dependent activity that is still relatively responsive to individual and community decision. The construction industry itself is localized. Homes are often built by the people who occupy them. Consequently, change in architecture can occur on a piecemeal basis without the need for global systems decisions involving the whole of society.

Nevertheless, the most significant change in American architecture over the last century has been the growing dependence of American homes on centralized, technological infrastructures for the provision of food, fuel, water and building materials. To provide these foods and services the technological infrastructures are, in turn, exploiting resources on a planetary basis. The net result has been to make homes extremely vulnerable to any global crisis or systems instability. This would not matter so much if the planetary picture were rosy, but as we all know too well, it is not. Serious doubt has been cast on our ability to maintain present rates of growth into the future on a planetary basis if this growth is on a "straight-through" fossil fuel technology that extracts, processes, distributes and consumes goods derived from a limited resource base without regard for thermodynamics, biological processes or basic resource constraints themselves. As many people have pointed out, there is real need to develop an "equilibrium technology" that recognizes human culture and environmental processes as being two coupled and mutually adaptive systems open to evolution and growth within these basic constraints.

The principal requirements are becoming increasingly obvious, and time is putting its own date on their necessity: a shift from fossil fuels to alternative energy sources, such as solar, geothermal and possibly nuclear; an improvement in overall energy-utilization efficiency from the current 15 to 20 percent to at least 45 percent; the development of biologically stable, soil-enhancing, productive and energy-efficient food production methods (currently U.S. agriculture is a net consumer rather than producer of energy); the build-up of two-to-five year stores of food, energy, water and essential raw materials (present world food reserves are sufficient for twenty-three days at subsistence level, or about the time it would take to distribute them); population stabilization at current levels nationally and at not more than 2.5 times present size globally; materials recycling up to the energy-economic limit with a 70 percent recovery of scarce or high energy materials before the end of the century; the elimination or control of local and global pollution so that it remains within the handling capacity of natural cycles.

These requirements are easy to enumerate but extremely difficult to achieve. Nevertheless, we may be witnessing the beginnings of a solar society today. A combination of photovoltaic, solar, tidal, geothermal and bioconverted energy, in conjunction with fuel cells, improved batteries, thermal storage and integrated energy systems could feasibly provide 80 percent of U.S. energy requirements within a century. The scientific and ecological rewards of doing so would be tremendous. The shift from a fossil-fuel-based economy to one that is powered for the most part by natural energy sources may well prove to be the most important development in Western technology since the advent of the coal-based industrial revolution.

*Solar energy suffers from premature economic assessments based on the kind of short-term thinking that got us into our present predicament*

Presently solar energy suffers from a surfeit of premature and largely irrelevant economic assessments that are based on exactly the kind of short-term thinking that got us into our present predicament in the first place. The basic point at issue is not the comparison of today's fossil fuel prices with the costs of the latest six-month-old collector but the necessity of an eco-compatible energy base for technological society, starting with the housing stock. It is sobering to speculate that if all the money spent to date on nuclear research had been invested in solar collectors at $5.00 per square foot, nearly 30 percent of the existing housing stock would already be solarized. Of all the great technological efforts that the U.S. has undertaken, such as the Manhattan and Apollo Projects, the Solar Project may yet turn out to be the most valuable.

In any case, it is difficult to imagine how it would be possible to move towards an equilibrium technology without some major changes in architecture. On the contrary, I will argue that the built environment is the logical starting point.

I believe that we are moving towards a "soft," symbiotic architecture that is grown rather than built, an integrated architecture based as much on information processing, bio-design and solar energy as it is on the articulation of materials and spaces.

Of all elements of the built environment the home is distinguished as being a microcosm of the macrocosm it is set in. It reflects, on the level of the biological unit, the same needs that society as a whole exists to provide. By changing the house we inevitably change society. A society's architecture is the one element of the sociotechnological system that is the most amenable to change. What cannot be changed from the top may perhaps be changed from the bottom. Your home is your biosphere.

Taking this approach, we can apply much the same criteria to the home as suggested for society as a whole. The object becomes to develop a home that is heated and cooled by natural energy, grows 70 percent of its food requirements and recycles most of its wastes. This implies a shift in domestic architecture from the Le Corbusian paradigm of the modern home as a "machine-for-living"—a direct extension of fossil-fuel powered technological society—to the concept of architecture as an extension of the natural environment fueled by the same forces that drive the rest of the biosphere.

Such a concept is not as utopian as it might appear; the energy fluxes required are available in most of the more densely populated areas of the U.S.A., and the technology required to utilize them is rapidly being developed. The main problems are economic rather than theoretical. In fact, a number of potential bioshelters have already been built, as witnessed by John Todd's Ark (New Alchemy Institute), David Holloway's Ouroboros House (University of Minnesota) and the Olkowskis' Integral House in Berkeley (Farallones Institute).

World-wide, a great many people and institutions are working at all levels to create the technologies that will make an organic, negentropic architecture possible. Few, however, would claim that the means for residential autonomy are already available. In fact, even when developed they may remain uneconomic at anything less than a community scale. The main stumbling blocks lie in developing decentralized high energy sources for electrical generation, cooking and refrigeration, i.e., for functions requiring high thermodynamic availability. It is much easier to develop low grade energy sources than high grade ones. Even more serious is the inadequacy of all current forms of energy storage, chemical, thermal or kinetic, to handle the sporadic, diurnal or seasonal nature of biospheric energy cycles. Efficient energy storage is a fundamental necessity in an uncertain world, be it for food crops, thermal energy, water or electricity. It is our only real insurance against tomorrow.

If one were foolish enough to envision the Garden of Eden as a habitat having a 70 degrees F. year-round temperature, then four inventions are necessary for its realization: a night sky radiating weather-skin, a transparent insulation, a material that changes from transparent to reflective when heated above a specified temperature point and a phase-change heat storage system. Together these four materials make it possible to maintain an enclosed microclimate within a few degrees of 70 year-round in the lower three fourths of the U.S.A.

Although the analogy is far from exact, a climatic envelope can be viewed as an attempt to reduplicate the way the Earth itself arrives at thermal equilibrium using thin-films of special materials. The transparent insulation is analogous to the Earth's atmosphere, which transmits solar energy but is relatively opaque to longwave heat radiation. The heat sensitive transparent/reflective material can be compared to very convenient clouds which only gather when it is too hot—which is why Day Chahroudi dubbed it "Cloud Gel." The heat storage material plays the same role in relation to heat storage as the Earth's land masses and oceans. When the material is heated above 75 degrees F., it absorbs the sun's energy as latent heat which it subsequently gives up at night when the interior temperature drops. In the summer the same heat storage systems can be used to store "cool." Finally, the infrared transparent weather-skin allows excess heat to radiate to space, the final heat sink for all thermal processes on Earth.

The envelope works by letting in solar energy when the interior temperature is below 73 degrees F., heating up both the interior and the phase-change heat storage materials. At night the transparent insulation prevents most of the daytime heat gain from escaping, and what heat does escape is compensated for by heat that is released from storage. Only when the "Thermocrete" is fully charged with three to five days worth of heat does the interior temperature begin to rise. This rise in interior temperature causes the whole envelope to change color from a transparent blue to an opalescent white as the Cloud Gel switches from transparent to reflective. This cuts down the heat gain to a fraction of its former value.

On summer nights warm air from the interior is allowed to rise up behind the Cloud Gel and transparent insulation and warm a radiating plate which radiates to the cool night sky. The cooled air falls and gives up its coolness to the Thermocrete which stores it for use during the next day. In this way the climatic envelope maintains a constant year-round temperature both summer and winter. It does this automatically and without using any moving parts other than on the molecular level.

*If all the money spent to date on nuclear research had been invested in solar collectors, nearly 30 percent of the existing housing stock would already be solarized*

A homeostatically regulated microclimate gives the base conditions required for a year-round growing season. A year-round growing season makes possible the development of a self-sustaining, integrated ecosystem with a net productivity sufficient to meet most nutritional needs. A biological habitat heated and cooled by the sun is the equivalent of a guaranteed minimum standard of living.

The first practical application of the climatic envelope technology was the installation of a transparent insulation using Suntek's Solar Membrane in a small greenhouse at the New Alchemy Institute on Cape Cod. Currently, arrangements are being made to produce all the required materials, with the exception of the night sky radiating weather-skin, on a commercial scale. The overall costs are estimated to be $7.50 per square foot.

Climatic envelopes will enable us to air-condition a whole building complex or even an entire city. A complex of variously shaped and sized envelopes that include both open and enclosed spaces would maximize diversity while minimizing climatic impacts. The articulation of the envelope can avail itself of the full range of the wide-span, light-weight structural vocabulary that has emerged during the last three decades, ranging through

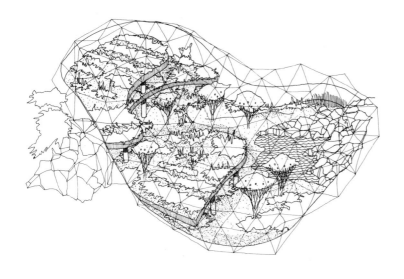

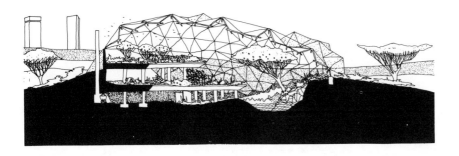

inflated and tensile structures, thin shells, folded plates, space frames and geodesics.

Activities which at present are housed only for climatic reasons could take place in the "open air." The "internal" architecture would not be subject to wind loads, snow loads, rain or large thermal variations. It can be as sculptural, as flexible or as unassuming as the situation calls for. Climatic envelopes make a "Polynesian" style architecture that is almost an extension of gardening. One can imagine tropical parks in Illinois, covered campuses and shopping malls with orange trees in Massachusetts or enclosed garden residences with an almost invisible internal architecture.

Sean Wellesley-Miller      89

Climatic envelopes reduce the land area needed by a self-sustaining ecosystem capable of supporting a family of four from about ten acres in the natural state to approximately one-half to one-fourth acre. This is still too large to be economic. A bioshelter attempts to reduce this area to about one thousand square feet or less. To do this, some of the criteria have to be relaxed, and the domestic ecosystem becomes a much more tightly programmed and energy-intensive one.

These and other considerations led us at Suntek to explore some radically different approaches to solar climate control in addition to the by-now-familiar flat-plate solar collector, thermal storage unit and back-up system that presently constitute a solar building.

The Bioshelter I figure shows the solar and heat transfer mechanisms of a "mobile home" bioshelter designed for retired people as New Age pioneers.

**Bioshelter I**

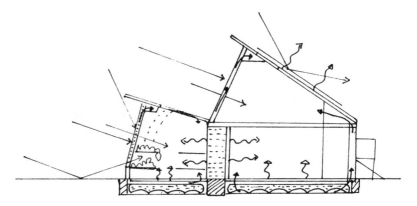

The building's windows, walls and roof are treated as "energy surfaces" designed to take maximum advantage of summer and winter energy fluxes. Thus the greenhouse glazing is angled for maximum winter sun penetration and the upper collectors for year round collection, while the roof is sloped and colored to reflect summer sun. The north wall is minimized to cut down heat loss.

The key solar heating elements are the greenhouse, the high temperature collectors and the heat storage systems. This particular design is shaped to provide 80 percent or more of the space heating required in a Boston climate. The high temperature collectors run a freezer for long term food storage and provide solar heated hot water. No attempt is made to generate electricity for lighting and electrical appliances or biogas for cooking because economic analysis proved these to be so expensive as to raise the price of a bioshelter above the $30,000 target set. If attempted at all, they are best done on a community scale.

Besides being designed for solar heating and cooking, the Bioshelter also has food chains, water recycling systems, biological waste treatment and the attendant control functions built into the architecture. Physiology reflects metabolism.

In many ways the heart of the system is the greenhouse, composed of the climatic envelope materials, which acts as humidifier, potable water still and solar collector, as well as producing fresh fruit and vegetables, mushrooms and flowers. Following a suggestion of Day Chahroudi, who was responsible for much of the early thinking on self-sufficient homes, the greenhouse is divided into three sections in which humidity and other microclimatic variables can be cycled independently to optimize plant growth conditions and discourage the spread of aphids and fungi.

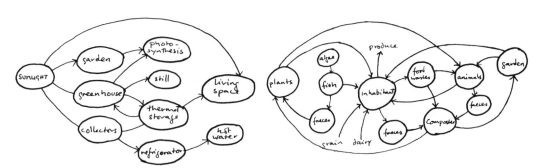

**Bioshelter I: Energy flows and Food chains**

A bioshelter recognizes interconnectedness. Although it is not a completely closed system, it is a tightly looped one with multiple functions superimposed on the same system components and with each system component interacting to a varying degree with every other component. Thus the water storage tubes function both as heat storage elements and aquaculture ponds and are connected with the greenhouse not only through heat exchange mechanisms but also by food and nutrient loops; fish wastes are used as

Sean Wellesley-Miller     91

nutrients for the plant beds and some plants are used to augment the algae diet of the fish. This is represented in a simplified way by the bio-loop diagrams showing the energy flows, food chains and water cycles.

**Bioshelter I:
Water cycle**

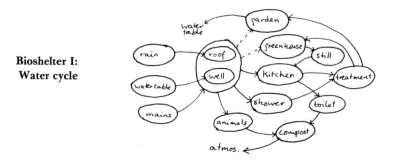

Each arrow does not necessarily represent a pipe or a continuous flow, nor is the system completely self-regenerating. Fish fingerlings, chicks and some seedlings would be purchased from outside community centers. Nevertheless, simulations of the model show that approximately 75 percent of the food supply for three people could be produced by the system. The principle outside purchases are grains and dairy products which may be partially paid for by the sale of excess produce.

The key to the waste handling system is the Clivus Multrum composter, a highly complex ecology all on its own. The only one I have been at all intimate with was so alive that I was tempted to call it "Clive." Literally millions of insects and bacteria were working in harmony to reduce wastes to sterile, soil-enhancing humus in an environment highly hostile to pathogens. A Clivus toilet is a major feat of applied biological engineering that disentangles water, solid wastes and organic matter with an elegant solution based on the way nature herself does it. Nevertheless, other solutions may be preferable in the future if their costs can be reduced and efficiency raised. The most attractive from a closed system viewpoint would be methane generation on a community scale for cooking. It would tie in naturally with community dairy farming and hog raising.

The water-cycle diagram shows the bio-loops involved in water treatment. In areas with an abundance of water a much simpler system could be used. In fact, each of the major bio-systems would in practice be adapted to local circumstances. Bioshelters in remote areas with steady wind speeds might employ wind turbines. Others in areas like Vermont or Oregon would tend to rely on seasonal heat storage and efficient wood burning stoves. Bioshelters in water scarce areas such as the Southwest would pay much more attention to water conservation and have simpler solar systems.

As advances occur in heat storage, photovoltaics, battery technology and microprocessing, so the overall systems configuration will change. Within a century it will probably be possible to build inexpensive and completely self-sufficient homes anywhere in the U.S.A. Moreover, homes may well become net producers of food and energy.

As buildings develop what one might call an integrated metabolism, there will be a natural tendency for them to develop "nervous systems" to regulate them. Microprocessors are already controlling the heating and cooling modes of solar buildings. Before long, household minicomputers may be suggesting greenhouse planting schedules and nutritionally balanced menus based on current ecosystem output, reporting on overall systems status in relation to expected weather patterns and keeping household accounts, as well as watering the plants and feeding the animals. Domestic minicomputers tied into community information nets will be able to say who is available for baby-sitting, match up passengers in the electric car pool and arrange produce swaps. The possibilities are nearly endless.

As we move into a solar architecture so we will move into a different everyday experience of time and space. We will switch from clock time to bio-time, recognizing the rhythm of seasons and the cycles of growth and decay. Our ideas of structure will become more organic and less mechanical. The interface between interior and exterior will become active and transformational rather than passive or isolating, softer and more subtle to the point where the architecture of residential ecology merges with its natural setting.

Architecture will almost literally become alive, responding like an organism to changes in its internal and external environment. Its future evolution will entail transformations in physiology and metabolism and, almost inevitably, the development of what one is tempted to describe as an autonomic nervous system to

*Architecture will almost literally become alive, responding like an organism to changes in its internal and external environment*

Sean Wellesley-Miller          93

regulate energy flows and biological processes. Solar energy, ecology and information processing are the three keystones of such an architectural future and are likely to have as much impact on the way architecture looks and functions as the development of concrete, glass and steel, together with the automobile and artificial lighting, did on the architecture of the 1920s.

The metamorphosis of the home into a solar powered "domestic ecosystem" will, nevertheless, place its own constraints on form and function. The new paradigm must and will find its own contextual conformities that may well lead to the rebirth of regional architectures adapted to local climates, materials and life styles.

In a more immediate time frame, the real challenge will be to make solar heating and integrated food production through greenhousing applicable to existing buildings, urban, suburban and rural, both in the U.S. and abroad. The hard fact remains that even if 70 percent of all new buildings constructed between now and the end of the century are solar heated and cooled most buildings will still be dependent on other sources of energy in the year 2000.

The bioshelter and climatic envelope concepts described here are only particular and partial attempts at broaching some of the problems presented by the architecture of our situation. Their biggest weakness is perhaps their very self-containedness. Ultimately, our responsibility for the natural environment is a collective one. To be really effective, bio-design will have to be instigated at the community and regional levels. Perhaps a first step towards this would be the development of community and bio-regional stability indicators that measure how far a particular area, defined in terms of its ecology, climate and culture, currently is from primary self-sufficiency in terms of the basic necessities of food, water and energy. In many regions of the country I suspect this goal could be achieved, or the situation improved dramatically, with a relatively small effort. What is lacking is the attempt; the means are emerging with a surprising rapidity, and the solarization of architecture is central to them.

95

E.F. Schumacher was born in Germany and educated at Columbia and Oxford. Although he has been the top economist on the British Coal Board and an adviser to the government of Burma, he is far from an orthodox thinker, as he demonstrates in his bestselling Small is Beautiful: Economics as if People Mattered. He is the founder and chairman of the Intermediate Technology Development Group in London, which works with developing countries on appropriate technology.

Dr. Schumacher
inside
New Alchemy's
dome-pond fish farm

# A Metaphysical Basis
# 8 For Decentralization

# E.F. Schumacher

If we are going to talk about decentralization we should give this some sort of metaphysical basis, because without a metaphysical basis any subject, outside the natural sciences, has no meaning at all. This means that we have to begin with some pretty wide concepts. The concepts I wish to start with I've written on the blackboard. There you see the word "unity"; underneath "diversity" and "multiplicity"; and still lower down "uniformity."

Well, we are all familiar with the middle terms. We find vast diversity and multiplicity in nature, in society, and in ourselves, a great variety. When we approve of this variety we normally call it diversity and when we are a bit fed up with it we call it multiplicity. "You can't have all this multiplicity!"

We are also sadly familiar with the bottom term—uniformity—because it reflects the main tendency of the modern world. It's what the modern world imposes on nature; for instance, agriculture has now become a monoculture that exhausts the soil and diminishes the gene pool. It's also imposed in society through monster organizations, monstrous production units, mass production, standardization, mechanization and, with man, mass education. In fact (I owe this insight to Ivan Illich), the mass production of people through mass education, compulsory mass education, was introduced a hundred years before industrial mass production was introduced.

Now, what I particularly want to emphasize is that unity and uniformity seem to look very much alike. So the most important thing is that we should train our minds, train our eyes, to distinguish between unity and uniformity.

But what do we mean by unity? This is the level, if I may put it that way, with which we are least acquainted. Unity is difficult to attain, it's very difficult to attain inside ourselves. Even a saint like St. Paul had to struggle against this lack of unity inside himself: "For the good that I would, I do not: but the evil which I would not, that I do. Oh wretched man that I am! With the mind, I myself serve the law of God, with the flesh, the law of sin."

Unity has something to do with God.

And diversity and multiplicity have something to do with our Earth.

And uniformity has something to do with Hell.

The difference, although the words sound much the same, between unity and uniformity is the greatest possible difference. But, as you know and as our forefathers knew, Satan is the ape of God. So our main efforts must be to try to distinguish which way we are going, because this middle condition, the earthly condition of multiplicity, is intrinsically a very unstable condition, unstable, troublesome, strenuous, uncertain, dangerous, potentially violent—and today I should say inflationary. It's a condition that one always wishes to get out of. It causes a sort of existential anguish.

There are two ways of getting out of it, the upward way to God, or the downward way into Hell. For "up" one can say "inner"; for "down" one can say "outer." (But we haven't really time to go into all the terminological problems that are raised immediately when one talks about these things.) The upward movement may be made impossible, for instance, by the belief that man is nothing but an outcome of mindless evolution. This is the sort of thing that we learn from Nobel Prize winners like Jacques Monod in his book **Chance and Necessity.** If these people are right, then there is only one way out of this existential anguish of multiplicity, namely, into uniformity, which is, as I said, the ape of unity.

Going a little bit further, we can make a number of additional associations. Unity, the level of God as it were, let's associate with the concept of quality and, if you like, with the concept of the spiritual. The bottom level, there's no doubt, we have to associate with the concept of quantity and in a certain sense with the concept of the material. And in the middle we have a mixture of the two. I want you particularly to think about the quantity and quality. Of course, pure quality without any quantity at all (i.e., pure spirit without any body, without any matter), on the one hand, and, on the other hand, pure quantity without any qualitative determination (i.e., pure matter without any spiritual content) do not exist in manifestation. They are beyond manifestation.

I don't know if any of you know the works of René Guénon; his last book was called **The Reign of Quantity.** As this reign of quantity increasingly establishes itself, we achieve ever-increasing uniformity and life becomes hell. When, or if, or as the reign of quantity is pushed away and the reign of quality comes in, then we move upwards towards unity, which as we know is also called ''the kingdom of God.''

Now, with this background, let us look at the problem of structure, centralization and decentralization. There can't be anything in manifestation, I mean ''extant on this Earth,'' without some structure, because everything must have some material components, and the more material it is, the more structure it requires. And the more immaterial it is, the less structure it requires. Centralization, as a movement, always means a simplification of structure, a reduction in the numbers of centers, the extreme being a monolith. Is centralization going to lead us upwards to the fulfillment of human destiny, or does it lead us down into Hell? Does it lead us towards unity or towards uniformity? The same questions hold if we talk about decentralization. Will the process, the attempt to decentralize, lead us into unity or away from unity or perhaps even into uniformity?

How do we decide whether it's going to lead us upwards or downwards? This is the crucial question. We first have to know **what** is being decentralized or centralized because there is a scale from the purely material to the purely immaterial. The greater the material, the greater is the relevance of quantity and the need for well articulated structures; the more immaterial, non-material, the smaller is the relevance of quantity. In fact, in the extreme, immaterial things are not quantitative and require no structure at all.

We can say, for instance, that when it comes to actual production — handling material, working in an actual physical situation — there quantity counts. There the number of people I am working with is a matter of decisive importance, because the number of people I can work with **as persons** is very limited. If there is one person, there is no relationship; I don't count my relation to myself as a relationship. If there are two of us, there's one relationship. If there are three of us, there are three relationships. If there are four of us, there are already six. If there are ten of us, there are forty-five. If there are twelve, there are sixty-six. Jesus evidently thought that was enough, that was all he could handle. When there are a hundred, there are 4,950 bilateral relationships. Who can carry those in his head? Then, for most people most others are no longer persons; they are just numbers. So if we work actually in the material, the physical realm, quantity counts tremendously — from the metaphysical point of view that I'm taking — because quantity, if excessive, suffocates. In other words (and all sociologists know this; they use the term ''primary work groups''), primary work groups are small. The general consensus is that Jesus was right; about a dozen is all one can handle.

When we come to relatively more immaterial things, not actual work but perhaps ideas, then of course quantity doesn't enter. And quantity can't suffocate. So this is quite a different matter. We don't dehumanize an idea if the idea is communicated to all mankind.

How many centers are required? At the extreme, at the top, the purely spiritual level, there is only one center, the Divine. In work with people and materials on this earth, however, there need to be very many centers, or else we get involved in bigness beyond the human scale, which inevitably tends to uniformity. With ideas, bigness, universality, worldwide impact, provided the ideas are good, can lead to unity. (If they are bad, they probably also lead to uniformity, but that is another matter.) With material things, enough is enough, and there are limits to growth. With ideal things, immaterial things, matters of the mind, the heart, the spirit, the very concept of enough is inapplicable (because it's a purely quantitative concept), and there are no limits to growth. To speak about limits to growth there is meaningless.

So where do we need many centers and where do we not need many centers? That is the question of decentralization and centralization. I think I have at least given some indication of my own thinking: the answer must be in accordance with the position on this scale—from the crudest material to the highest spiritual. The position of every person, every one of us, is that we need on the one hand to be able to do our own thing, even letting each one of us be a center, the power of doing being centralized to me, to you. At the same time, as spiritual beings, we have only one orientation, to only one center; only if we have this orientation can we achieve the brotherhood of men, if you permit such a sentimental sounding but very meaningful word. So at one level, we need to be split up into many, many groups, while unity can be achieved only by some higher power that coordinates the thinking, feeling and striving of these groups. It cannot be done by material organization. To put it another way, material things necessarily have frontiers. Without frontiers they couldn't exist; they would be everywhere and nowhere, whereas ideas have no frontiers.

Now what follows from all this is that we must get away from asking whether centralization is a Good Thing or decentralization is a Good Thing. We have to be very precise about it. One of the great teachers of the western world, Thomas Aquinas, started every second one of his paragraphs with the word **distinguo**. First of all let's distinguish **what** we are going to centralize or decentralize. To strive for unity on the ideal plane, for instance the universality of the rule of law, is one thing. But it does not follow that we would get anything but dreadful uniformity if we tried this on the physical plane—if, for instance, we translated this lightheartedly into material arrangements, thinking that a "world state" would solve our problems. It may be valid to say that once a really good thing has been invented such knowledge should be universally available and, maybe, universally applied. But to say that production should be centralized, as is the tendency of the modern world with multinational corporations and so on, is quite a different kettle of fish.

Let's start again and try to encircle the problem in another way. I know the approach I am about to take has become exceedingly unpopular, but not, I trust, in this group. After all, everything we do and talk about should be orientated to, and derived from, an answer to the question, "Why are we here in this world anyhow?" It is not all that pleasant to be here and it's for a very short time. What's the point of it? Life actually, for most of us, is too short to find out on our own. But luckily, we have not been left without guidance. This guidance is in fact manifest through the religious traditions of mankind. We have the inestimable benefit today that knowledge of all religions has become accessible, even in paperbacks. We don't have to be immensely learned; it's all available in translations. And if we pay attention to it we find, as was pointed out here yesterday, a great Convergence. Not that the religions themselves are converging, because truth is truth—and truth doesn't "converge." But our understanding, with deeper insight, is that where it matters they all teach the same.

And what do they teach? I will put it in the language of a great Christian saint, who wrote a very famous book in which he started by laying The Foundation. And The Foundation says this: "Man was created to praise, reverence and serve God our Lord and by this means to save his soul. And the other things on the face of the Earth were created for man's sake and in order to aid him in the prosecution of the end for which he, man, was created." And then with the most precise logic, it goes on to say, "From which it follows that man ought to make use of these other things just so far as they help him attain his end and that he ought to withdraw from them just so far as they hinder him."

This is a saint talking, not a businessman. Of course a businessman, if he has any sense, says exactly the same. He first determines what he is trying to do and then uses the means of his environment just so far as it helps him to do it—and he draws back the moment he finds he is doing so much that it hinders him. The logic is impeccable.

All the same, to the modern world and to many of us, or to many strong parts inside us, this is a totally unacceptable prescription. But perhaps the real predicament we find ourselves in, particularly in those countries that can totally disregard this rule, is precisely due to the disregard of this rule. We are not using the facilities the Creator has put at our disposal for the purpose of attaining an end. We don't even think about what our end is. We're using things only because they're there. Our engineers and scientists produce something more we could use, so we must use it. It's got nothing to do with any clear purpose of man to save his soul, or anything else, to land people on the moon, or if someone has come to such a condition that his heart is totally ruined, to make a heart transplant. But we do these things because it's possible to do them.

We're a society that's rich in means and poor in purpose.

(I wasn't all that much against the moon landings. I had myself quite a list of people to send, but when I found they always fetched them back again, I thought it was completely purposeless.)

So from this point of view—that there is a purpose in human life and that we are entitled to use the means of the world just as far as we need them to attain this purpose but should withdraw from them when they begin to hinder us—it is impossible to take any interest in a discussion of economic growth. And it's equally impossible to get excited if somebody says non-growth or zero-growth; these are purely quantitative concepts and therefore have no intelligible meaning at all. It is quite amazing how difficult it is to convince even well-meaning people that it is depraved to argue about growth or non-growth, that such an argument misses out on everything that matters. A purely quantitative concept only fits at the level of uniformity, of Hell. Is physical growth a good thing? Well, when my children grow, this is exactly as it should be, but if I would suddenly start to grow, it would be a disaster. So is growth Good or is it Bad? Is decentralization or centralization Good or Bad? These are empty, purely quantitative concepts.

So that's the first point. We are not interested in growth or non-growth. We are interested that that which is required and healthy and good should grow and that that which is not required, unhealthy and evil should diminish. Whether the addition of these two processes (which evil-minded statisticians make, to end up with GNP), whether that GNP rises or falls should be of no concern to anybody who has any sense whatever.

Now the second point. Our chairman disclosed that I spent a number of years as a farm laborer. One of my jobs was to go every morning before breakfast "to yonder hills" and count the cattle in the field. And I did this half asleep, went back to the farm, touched my cap to the bailiff and said, "Yes, sir, thirty-two." And he said, "Go and have your breakfast." One day when I arrived at the field there was an old farmer leaning on the gate, and he said, "Young man, what do you do here every morning?" This was war time; maybe he thought I was a spy. I said, "I do nothing; I mean, I just count the cattle." He shook his old head and said, "If you count them every day they won't flourish." So I trotted back thinking, "How stupid can they get?" I mean, he said this to a professional statistician; after all! Then one day I arrived at the field and I counted and counted again. There were only thirty-one. Well, I wanted my breakfast. I went back, touched my cap and told the bailiff, "There are only thirty-one," "That's bad," he said. "Go and have your breakfast and we'll go there together." We went together, we searched the place, and there was a dead beast under one of the bushes. I said to myself, "Why have I been counting them all the time? The thing has died. It would also have died if I had never been there, for all I know."

*If you mainly direct your mind to the quantitative aspects, you're getting down into Hell*

Then I got for the first time a glimpse of what is meant by the universal tradition of all peoples — all dutifully collected in a book by Sir James Fraser, **The Sin of Statistics** — that if you mainly direct your mind to the quantitative aspects, you're getting down into Hell. You're treating everything as units, as uniform, and you don't notice the qualitative things that really matter, that make or mar things — namely to look at each beast with qualitative understanding and say, "Well, this one looks a bit mingey."

A farm laborer in Scotland was asked by the boss to count the sheep. He had them all in the sheep pen and then they rushed out. After they'd all left, the boss asked, "Well, how many are there?" The laborer said, "I don't know, but I know the one that is missing.'' You see, he even knew his sheep one by one; he didn't have to count them. He missed a friend and that is far more real information than thirty-two or thirty-one. Unless we become interested in the qualitative meaning of things, we're wasting our time—we are leading the whole thing down into Hell.

Of course we cannot totally disregard quantity. Sometimes we can make figures sing, and that is the real task of a statistician. You will not catch me producing big tabulations, because they don't sing. But you do catch me producing what I would consider significant figures where the quality expresses itself in the quantity. Consider, for example, the distribution of income in the world. If you take normal distribution of anything, you get the well-known Gaussian bell shaped curve—a few at one extreme (there are always some stragglers), a few at the other extreme (there are always some geniuses or exceptionally greedy people), but most people are in the middle. But if you take the world distribution of income today, you get an inverted Gaussian curve. That is to say, there are very, very many people extremely poor, very many people extremely rich, and hardly anybody in the middle. You can see there the quality of the distribution; it's a pathological distribution. That is to say, there is not one world anymore; even on that humble level any semblance of unity has been lost. And this doesn't merely apply between the rich countries and the poor countries (where it applies in a horrifying form); it also applies inside many societies. All the developing countries are becoming ever more dual societies, with a lot of people immensely poor, a few people immensely rich, and nothing in the middle. If you link this up with ''The Foundation'' that I've quoted, evidently some people don't observe the idea that they have other purposes in life than the material. To put it into the shorthand of Christian language, their job is really to save their souls and they are using far more of the material means than is necessary for this purpose. Therefore, it's most likely that they are greatly hindered and won't save their souls.

So we see that the rich society, that is to say the people at the rich end, cannot possibly be a model for the world as a whole. And unless we find a new model we are just going to drift deeper and deeper into disaster. The rich society norm says to the world at large, ''If only you adopt our technology and our methods, you can all live like little Americans or little Western Europeans or little Japanese.'' That is just plain nonsense. It can't be. A different model is required—we might say a culture of poverty.

Now all the culture that we have comes from a culture of poverty. If you go to Chartres or to Durham or anywhere, a thousand places, or to the Taj Mahal, you find that our ancestors have been able to do cultural things that we can't rival; we can't rival them economically. That's the extraordinary thing—we can't even afford them. Our affluence is so immensely wasteful on the ephemeral side that on anything permanent, like building something splendid, we can't afford it. We subject everything, even that which we mean to do for eternity or for permanence, to an economic calculus, which is a contradiction in terms.

I had the privilege of going to Florence only a year ago, and I looked at the cathedral there. Opposite the cathedral—this fantastic cathedral!—there is a statue of the architect. His name is Arnulfo, and he looks admiringly at his work. On the pedestal is a Latin inscription, which with the greatest difficulty I deciphered, and it said: ''This is Arnulfo, who, instructed by the municipality of Florence to build a cathedral of such splendor that no human genius can ever surpass it, on account of the splendid endowment of his mind, proved equal to this gigantic task.'' It does not say ''instructed by the Medicis.'' This was the republic of Florence, in the preindustrial age when GNP was such a tiny fraction of what it is now in this country or even in Italy that we would say, ''Well, they must have perished!—How could they build such a thing?'' They didn't apply the economic calculus; they just did it. They instructed it should be done.

We have in a way advanced into Hell. I tried to imagine what it would look like if I found a statue of the architect opposite one of the highrise office block buildings in London. It would probably read: ''This is Mr. X.Y. Smith, member of the Royal Institute of British Architects, who, instructed by the Greater London Council to create an office block of such superlative cheapness per square foot that no human genius can ever underbid it, on account of his superb endowment with computers, proved equal to this mean task.''

We have put everything under some concept of efficiency. Of

course no one in his senses would be in favor of inefficiency. We are all in favor of efficiency, but the concept has become unbelievably narrow. It only considers one thing and that is efficiency in the most material aspect of the job. If I said this is a splendid process of production and a very efficient process because it makes the workers happy, people would say, "Well, what's the matter with him? He must be a sentimental fool." I must prove that the workers work better or work faster or do better quality work in their happiness. If I can't prove that, then happiness doesn't count.

This of course has been noticed for a long time. The warnings have gone unheard. I'll read one of the classical statements from an encyclical by Pope Pius XI: "With the leaders of business abandoning the true path it was easy for the working class also to fall into the same abyss." (If you ask me what is the cause of inflation, this is it. Very many employers have treated their workers as mere tools.) "So bodily labor, which, after original sin, was decreed by Providence for the good of Man's body and soul, has in many instances been changed into an instrument of perversion." And then the encyclical has this, to me, terrible, sentence: "From the factory dead matter goes out improved, whereas men there are corrupted and degraded."

"From the factory dead matter goes out improved, whereas men there are corrupted and degraded"
—Pope Pius XI

I'm not saying that people are not aware of this situation, but they take it as a law of nature. There's a total immobility; there's just a little bit of tinkering. It is treated the same way that slavery was treated until it was abolished. Of course we want to be kind to the worker. Of course we realize we must do something; we must treat them with respect, and if they physically come to grief, then we must pay some compensation. If they mentally or spiritually come to grief we couldn't care less. The one thing we should understand is that compensation never compensates. Once the damage has been done, it cannot be undone.

So this concept, this very goods-oriented concept of efficiency, has led us into the whole mythology of the economies of scale. Hence, more specialization, more division of labor, more uniformity, more mindlessness—production becomes ever bigger, ever more complex, ever more capital intensive and, in a special sense, ever more violent. Well, you say, why is he telling us this? We know it all. I apologize, but the diagnosis is worth taking a little bit of time over. Where do we go from there?

E.F. Schumacher          107

Now, we have people who say we must change the system, and they're quite right, except one never knows what they mean. Society has produced this production system, but now the system molds society. It insists that every member of society respect the immanent logic of the system and adapt to it by accepting (that's the only way you can adapt, by accepting) its implicit aims as one's own. The first commandment is, "Thou shalt adapt thyself." In this sense man becomes captive of the system whether he approves of its aims or not. He cannot effectively adopt different aims and values (he can verbally do it, but not effectively) unless he takes steps to alter the system of production. In other words, ideas can change the world only by some process of incarnation.

The prevailing concept of efficiency rules the modern world, not by itself, but by the type of technology and the type of organization it has produced. The mere change of the concept is not enough. Unless and until some people have actually got down to work and have produced new types of work, new technologies, new types of organizations, new patterns of consumption, new patterns of distribution of the population—until that has happened—all the preaching (which is also necessary), all the appeals to people's goodness, their good sense, their ethical and spiritual qualities will invariably stay inside the system and will be powerless to alter the system. The system will not be altered unless there is a viable incarnation. We are taught, "In the beginning was the Word." But read on, read on. "It was made flesh and dwelled among us." A new concept will not be recognized or accepted and, of course, will be called impractical or even subversive. But whether it will eventually succeed in changing the world will depend not simply on its intrinsic truth but on the work it manages to manifest in the flesh.

*The system will not be altered unless there is a viable incarnation*

Let's take a short look at what kind of work is needed. For work we have to have some guidelines, some orientation. I have come to the conclusion that the suicidal tendencies of the modern world, quite apart from their disastrous spiritual implications, can be summed up in four criteria. Any such listing is to some extent personal and arbitrary, but I would sum it up like this.

First of all, there is the tendency towards giantism, economies of scale, all that. Secondly (and all these are closely interconnected), there is the tendency towards an unbelievable complexity. No doubt you have seen cars where progress was represented by the fact that you did not have to subject yourself to the indignity of turning a little handle to wind the windows up and down; you pressed the button and bzzz, they were down. These things of course break down and then cost a lot to repair. Even the simplest things one can't do oneself anymore. Everything has become too complex. Thirdly, vast expense in terms of capital is required to start to do anything. And the fourth is a tendency towards ever-increasing violence in the very production process itself.

From this it follows that if we want to do this work, to incarnate a more humane, a more Christian idea of carrying on, we will have to look in the opposite direction and look not only with our eyes but also with our hands. Can't we make things small again, reduce them to the human scale, get away from this giantism? Does everything have to be so complex? Can't we revise our whole ideas of patterns of consumption in the direction of simplicity? Can't we use our brilliant technology to evolve methods of production where even the little fellow can help himself and you don't have to be rich or powerful in order just to start? And can't we go systematically, determinedly in the direction of non-violence rather than violence? Only with the help of such knowledge and such technology—and it's not only hardware, it's also software—can we create a system that would serve man, in the place of the present system which enslaves him. But of course this is said by me from a Christian point of view, where serving man may mean something very different from what it means from the point of view of a purely materialistic civilization.

So first of all, back to the human scale. I've already given the arithmetical example of how with increasing numbers the number of relationships increases exponentially. If you have a technology that is small then that technology can use small sources of energy—extremely relevant to the whole energy problem. You could heat this building with solar energy but you can't heat the Rockefeller Center with solar energy; it wouldn't even propel the lifts. If you have a small scale technology, of course most of your ecological problems disappear because nature has tolerance margins—little skirmishes she can deal with but not massive assaults. If you have a small-scale technology, and only if you have a small-scale technology, you can get a better distribution of population. The fact that roughly seventy per cent of the population of this country live in cities, which among them cover just over one per cent of the surface area of the country, entails enormous energy usage. But this cannot be overcome with the existing technology because it's been produced by the existing technology. So the precondition of any kind of decentralization of the population is a new concept of smaller towns and better structure—villages around the market center, market centers around the major town, ideally no major town more than a couple of hundred thousand or thereabouts (everything more is an encumbrance and doesn't serve the human spirit at all). I would say this would also be very relevant to the problem of population explosion because wherever communities have been small enough for the mind to encompass, they have behaved perfectly reasonably in matters of procreation. But there is no use talking about decentralization unless one incarnates it in the flesh and creates the wherewithal, the means of doing so.

Next, back to some inherent simplicity. Simplicity is of value in itself from a Christian point of view. We're here to do just as much as is necessary to serve our real purpose. This excessive sophistication, complexity and specialization produces, as has been foreseen for 150 years, people so narrow-minded and so bothered that they have no time to become wise. Life becomes a constant agitation and strain which crowds out the spirit. It was a great insight to me when I travelled from England via the United States to Burma. It struck me that life in England is relatively very agreeable. The pace is not excessive; it's kindly, it's safe. I came to America, which I love, but I was bothered by the nervous strain, the number of people on psychiatrists' couches and so on. Then I went to Burma and there I found life as it really ought to be—bags of time, great relaxation and happiness, the jolliest people you could possibly encounter. And then it struck me that the amount of time people have is in inverse proportion to the amount of labor-saving machinery they employ. After all, this country is cluttered with labor-saving machinery, and everybody lives under the most terrible pressure. England is sort of backward, and Burma has never embarked on this road.

The third item, namely capital cheapness, is of very profound political, sociological and psychological importance. If you have a

*This excessive sophistication, complexity and specialization produces people so narrow-minded and so bothered that they have no time to become wise*

possibility of making a living when you're not already rich, and of creating something, then lots of people are admitted to the dinner table who today are progressively excluded. Hence the unhappiness of the so-called developing countries; with this high technology they find that, in spite of political independence, they become more and more dependent because they are not already rich and powerful. They're caught and they suffer immediate effects in mass unemployment.

The final item, non-violence, is also a value in itself from a Christian point of view. Christianity tells us that life is a school in which we must learn patience and forbearance and that we will not practice these among ourselves if we don't practice them also in our relations with Mother Nature. In Burma, before I was there, there was a British military station, about twenty or thirty miles away from the town. In order to get the mail to the people there, the British authorities hired an Indian chap with a horse and coach to bring the mail. They were prepared to pay him for this but not his entire costs because the coach was fitted to take passengers, and the road from this military station to the town was a very busy road with lots and lots of people walking or ox carts very slowly moving along. The Indian plied his trade for a year; when the year was out he came back and said, "I can't go on doing it at that price." "Why not?" "Because I can't get any passengers." "Why can't you get passengers? The coach is convenient, there are plenty of people, the price is perfectly reasonable and they all have money. Well then (probably someone had been to Harvard Business School), let's ask the consumer." And so they asked the consumers, these people who were walking twenty miles in the hot sun, "Why don't you use the coach? It only costs a couple of rupees." They said, "Look at the horses. The horses shouldn't be pulling a coach; they should be out on grass. We would never demean ourselves to travel behind horses that are so ill kept. We'd rather walk." Now that is man as the crown of creation; he cannot claim any dignity unless he realizes that **noblesse oblige.** And that, I found, was the most universal attitude in this backward country, Burma. If man is not the crown of creation but merely a naked ape, then of course it's difficult to sell to him the idea of **noblesse oblige.** And he behaves accordingly.

Non-violence is particularly needed in agriculture; here I'm speaking to the converted, I'm quite sure. But it presupposes also a far more decentralized way of doing the job because the most productive factor, which I think I helped to establish as a concept in English discussion, is the TLC factor; when you really apply it, it's extremely productive. People ask each other who makes it, but TLC means tender loving care.

The violence of modern medicine hardly needs to be mentioned. A clever chap asked, "If an ancestor visited us today, what would he be more astonished at, the skill of our dentists or the rottenness of our teeth?" But instead of tackling the problem, which we know is a solvable problem, of letting children grow up with healthy teeth, we get this continuous escalation between greater and greater rottenness of the teeth and greater and greater skill of dentists. So we always have reason to be immensely grateful for the existence of dentists who ought not to exist at all.

*I would suggest that the possibilities of any real change, not in the talking but in the doing, can only come from small groups of people*

Now if you take all this together, then I would suggest that the possibilities of any real change, not in the talking but in the doing, can only come from small groups of people. In a sense, we don't really need a theory of decentralization. The dinosaurs will collapse under their own weight. Innovating minorities are always small and are **ipso facto** decentralized. If any one of us still expects any real help from big powerful organizations, I suggest he is wasting his time. These organizations are big and powerful precisely because they are not, in this sense, innovating. So the best thing to do is to forget them, or even better, if you are clever enough, to use them as milch cows.

The battle is being joined between two groups of people. (The people who think there's no problem are not a factor; they will die away.) The first group I call the people of the forward stampede. Their slogan is, "A breakthrough a day keeps the crisis at bay." They resort to any degree of violence; they launch Project Independence with a vast and horrifying nuclear program, no holds barred. They have, like the devil, all the most catchy tunes. But the others, I call them the homecomers, remember themselves; they remember what life is really about and they do this kind of work that I've been trying to describe.

Sometimes, more than sometimes, I'm accused either of optimism or of pessimism. Unfortunately, I don't know which is the case here. Most attacks that I am unduly optimistic in thinking that anything can be done, I'm sorry to say, come from very young people. Other people say I'm a pessimist because I know something about the subject and therefore know we can't go on as before, for any length of time. Today anyone who calls black black is called a pessimist and anyone who calls black white is called an optimist. But what we need are optimistic pessimists—that is to say, people who know the danger of our situation, which is beyond any argument for those who know their onions, who know the facts. No one can argue with me as far as the fuel situation is concerned. No one can really argue with an experienced ecologist as far as the ecological situation is concerned. So in that respect, I am a pessimist. But I'm an optimistic pessimist because I believe that there are now lots of things going on that make change possible. Materially it's no real problem. We can live on a small fraction of what we are living on now, as the culture of poverty, wherever it has existed, has amply demonstrated. The great thing about the really optimistic pessimists is that they are not work-shy and they don't stay at the level of talk, talk, talk. They actually get their hands dirty and do some work. Let's hope we can all graduate to that class.

Richard J. Barnet has taught at Yale and at the University of Mexico and was a State Department adviser during the Kennedy administration. He is the co-author of Global Reach: The Power of the Multinational Corporations and is the founder and co-director of the Institute for Policy Studies in Washington, D.C.

# The Fate of the
# 9 Multinational Corporation

## *Richard Barnet*

In **Global Reach** I give the example of the Bulova Watch Company, which, in order to avoid taxes, sends the parts of its watches on a 22,000 mile jet flight. This is an almost perfect illustration, though by no means a unique one, of how it is possible to build a whole political and economic structure using money as a criterion for efficiency. Global planning made it economical for Bulova to take advantage of a loophole in the U.S. tariff laws. Because American Samoa is technically American territory you can take watch parts that are put together in Switzerland, fly them around the world, bring them back, and show a profit on the balance sheet. You can go on for years and years convincing yourself that you have done something very clever. In a sense you have been very clever because, by the way in which the institutions are developed, the social costs generally get thrown off on the rest of the society. You are minimizing your taxes (which only means that somebody else is picking them up), and you are not investing in pollution control or research into alternative energy sources. But if you take energy as the real test this structure becomes incredibly inefficient.

What makes the global corporation unique and makes it different from the corporation in the past is that it probably is the only institution that can plan on a global scale. It's able to look around the world and to pick from its very specific point of view the places to go for the cheapest labor, to go for resources, and to develop markets. The internationalist rhetoric and the internationalist ideology of the global corporation are very real, because, for the purposes of global planning, national boundaries are not only not important, they are impediments. It's important to transcend any territorial obstructions to the three fundamental bases of the power of the corporation—free movement of information, free movement of capital, and free movement of technology. What's different and what's relatively new about the global corporation is that, since its dramatic rise in the mid-60's, it has been an institution which really judges its performance by the global balance sheet; therefore, it may deliberately operate at a loss in any particular part of the system. One reason that underdeveloped countries suffer such adverse effects from multinational corporate operations is that it's in the interest of the corporation's overall balance sheet to minimize its profit, to take out more than it puts in, in a particular place, and this loss is part of the process of global planning.

*"We just show the box. It's like a flag and everybody sees it and knows what it is"*

I got a real sense of how quixotic these planners are when I met Mr. Bickmore, the President of Nabisco. I interviewed maybe forty or fifty top corporate executives in the United States and abroad, but Mr. Bickmore was a particularly interesting character. To him, the idea of a satellite with an ad which could reach two or three billion potential munchers of Ritz crackers wasn't just a dream, it was a plan. It had a target date sometime in the early 1980's. It had been costed at something like eight million dollars for a thirty second spot—a lot of money but very cheap. I asked him what was really a very stupid question. When he said he was going to flash this ad all over the world I asked if there wasn't a language problem. He said, "No, we just show the box. It's like a flag and everybody sees it and knows what it is." Then he said, "I have this experience all the time. I go down to Latin America and I walk into the supermarkets and I hear people saying, 'Reetz, Reetz,' and it really does my heart a lot of good." About four weeks after this interview, I was in a remote village far from Mexico City with absolutely no one around. Suddenly on the horizon I see a man on a burro. He's coming closer and closer and the burro is laden with something and as he gets closer, no, it was...that's right.

Mr. Bickmore was also interesting because he illustrated another point about the multinational corporations. The **raison d'etre** of the multinational corporation is centralization, the ability to make decisions at a global level which allows you to send something to the factory in Portugal instead of the factory in Germany in order to minimize the costs or to take advantage of labor conditions, advantageous transportation, or tariff agreements. I think that the very essence of the multinational corporation is this highly centralized process. Yet because centralization has a bad name there's a great deal of decentralization preached in the system—the idea that really the various components make decisions for themselves. Many studies have shown that if, in fact, the system is decentralized the advantages inherent in the idea of a global corporation are lost. Mr. Bickmore really made this point when he told an anecdote about what happened when Nabisco decided to break into the Common Market. He said, "I went to Europe and checked into a hotel in Brussels and spent three days going around to all the local candy stores and bakeries and filling my briefcase with all the various things they had. Then I went back to the hotel and put them all out on the bed. I spent two days in that room just tasting what it was that they liked in that country, and by the end of two days I knew what it took to get into this market." In a world market, the growth of the corporation depends critically upon developing a certain standardization and homogenization of taste so that you can accomplish the economies of scale.

The whole basic theory of corporation growth is to take what you have produced in one situation and extend its life into another. This process is called "cross-subsidization" and is the same process by which conglomerates are developed. You take a commanding position in one market, and then you move either laterally into another sector of the economy or geographically across borders. You have a tremendous advantage over local industry or competitors because you have already gotten back your basic research and development costs. I think this process of cross-subsidization, extension of one advantage into new markets, is the heart of what is really the corporate religion. You can find

*The growth of the global corporation depends upon developing a homogenization of taste in order to accomplish the economies of scale*

Richard Barnet        117

all kinds of standard statements by corporate leaders about how growth is a way of life—"We must grow or die." Given the system of rewards, given the notion that you must continually increase not only profits but the very rate of profit by the process of extension, it's not possible to see yourself standing still. The whole opposition to the idea of steady-state economy or limits to growth is very fundamental and is a recognition of the way the industrial system has developed. This fundamental need for growth is particularly evident in oligopolistic competition where a few actors are competing for a share of the market. When you talk to these managers you see that they really sense themselves in a situation beyond their control.

You ask are they going to make it. I don't really see how. Taking a short-range view, there's a tremendous accumulation and concentration of power and it's proceeding very quickly. I'm sure all of you have seen projections that show that two hundred or three hundred multinational corporations may end up with 65 percent of the assets of the world. If you look at who makes the basic decisions about what resources get exploited and under what terms they get exploited and how they're transported and how they're used, it's clear that increasingly there's a smaller number of multinational corporations.

I think there are two really fundamental problems that face the corporation. The first is that global profit maximization increase or maintenance, or increase of shares of the market are virtually the only standards for this peculiar kind of global corporate planning. These criteria seem to me impossibly simplistic because they conflict with all kinds of political, cultural, and social forces. People have strong feelings about not wanting to be part of a global corporate culture that is really a network of enclaves within larger societies. I think the fundamental conflict between the simplicity of the corporate goal and the complexity of social goals that are tied to territorially based needs is one very serious problem. I think another one is the time frame; the global corporation thinks primarily in terms of the annual balance sheet or the quarterly statement. From the point of view of the corporation it would seem, even over ten or fifteen years, to be very poor planning to substitute fossil fuels for human energy in underdeveloped countries. It seems peculiar to use a society's scarcest instead of its most abundant resources. There are a number of other examples of conflict between the corporation's own short-range goals and its longer term interests. One is the work ethic. By celebrating labor saving as a goal and leisure as the reward for working hard, the corporation has completely undermined the work ethic.

Finally, I think that the corporation's real source of strength and unique power is also what will ultimately unite a very strange and varied coalition of interest against it. The mobility of a corporation conflicts with the lack of mobility of most people. The corporation's peculiar efficiencies and its ability to exploit economies of scale stem from its mobility. It can move production very quickly from a high wage area to a low wage area. It can take advantage of changes in interest rates and currency by shifting from one currency to another through very elaborate processes of trans-national currency movements. This mobility obviously creates very serious problems for the people who are rooted in territories, for the workers who lose their jobs. A corporation can develop alternative production sites simply by moving money from one part of the system to another, but the community that has grown up dependent on that corporation cannot move so easily.

I think that the corporation is beginning to create very serious management problems for managers of territorial-based communities all over the world, regardless of their political ideology. Brazil, which celebrated and even made itself a doormat for the multinational corporation by offering it the most advantageous kinds of arrangements and enticements, is now reversing its policy. The reason is, I think, that people are beginning to understand the real meaning of interdependence. A given territorial unit cannot be managed for traditional stability—its money supply can't be protected, its air can't be protected, its minimum employment level can't be assured—if the largest economic units operating on that territory are free to come and go as they wish on the basis of criteria that have very little to do with territory. If over fifty percent of an American corporation's profits, payroll, or assets are out of the country (as is the case with the energy companies), it doesn't think and act like an American company anymore. This is equally true for Japanese and German companies. Until very recently it was always assumed that the growth of these large corporations simply increased the power of the home-base country. Though that's still true to some extent, it's also true that there are some very fundamental problems for the home-base country. It's obvious that the global corporation really is simply a logical extension of a process of corporate growth. A corporation's move to Hong Kong is not qualitatively different from a corporation's move south from the mill towns of Massachusetts. The same basic process is occurring for the same reasons and is generally supported by the same kind of technological development. But the growth of the global corporation has shattered, in a very fundamental way, some of the basic myths of the society, like the myth of countervailing power. The growth of the global corporation has dealt a severe blow to each of the three basic sources of countervailing power in the United States—labor, diversity, and the market.

The bargaining power of labor has been very seriously undercut by corporate mobility. It's not just that a corporation can move away and go to Hong Kong or Taiwan. A corporation can keep a plant operating at a minimum level and transfer most of the production to some other country. The fear of the corporation's moving away has badly undercut labor's bargaining power, a fear reflected in the acceptance of wage reductions in a number of recent negotiations. Labor's real wages have declined over 8 percent in the last few years.

The second source of countervailing power, at least in theory, was that business was not a homogenous unit. There were real differences of interest between various parts of the industrial sector—north and south, agriculture and manufacturing, big business and little business—and a very small number of decision-makers didn't essentially dominate the whole industrial system. Now, through the process of concentration, most small business has disappeared or has been swallowed up by the large global corporations, and the same decision-makers are operating across various industrial sectors. Once there may have been some real conflict between insurance and banking and between different areas of the finance industry. Now, since the banking conglomerates, the same interests operate pretty much free from constraint by competition and government. In this country even though government regulation of business has always been pretty much industry-dominated (at least very sensitive to the interests and apparent needs of industry), there was some level of regulation (which reached its high point during the New Deal) to prevent the industrial system from becoming chaotic. The global corporation has undermined a process of government regulation which presupposed a self-contained national economy. Our labor laws, tax laws, and pollution control laws are all based on an assumption whose validity is contradicted by the daily planning of the global corporation.

Finally, I suppose that all of our theory rests to a greater or lesser extent on the existence of the market. The market has been dealt a blow by the process of concentration which has continually accelerated the whole process of oligopoly. This is one factor which I don't think is sufficiently appreciated. More and more of our transactions are intra-corporate transactions; that is, they take place within the confines of a single corporation. Maybe two thirds of all the economic transactions in the United States are taking place between a parent and a subsidiary. When, in effect, the buyer and seller are the same person, prices are set not for traditional reasons but for reasons that have absolutely nothing to do with the transaction. It has been documented that, in a good many cases, artificial prices are set—so-called transfer pricing for tax saving, for moving money from one country to another, for getting more profits out of the country than are allowed by law, for all kinds of reasons—and over-pricing occurs. For example, the prices of some drugs bear absolutely no relationship to a market.

*Maybe two thirds of all the economic transactions in the United States are taking place between a parent and a subsidiary*

The global corporation has brought about a rather basic economic transformation and a crisis of values. Ultimately, I believe that the global corporation cannot really survive, both because of the energy problem and because it is fundamentally impossible to reconcile a global institution having such a narrow set of goals with minimal survival requirements. These conflicts are already becoming much more obvious. There is now a certain sense of crisis in the corporation itself. In the speeches of corporate leaders eight or nine years ago there was a kind of wild euphoria. These leaders were the prophets of the new world in which peace and abundance would be filtered through the system and made available to everybody. Now they have doubts about all that and haven't even been able to figure out a legitimatizing principle for the global corporation. This failure is, perhaps, the most serious crisis of all.

Richard Barnet 121

Saul Mendlovitz is a Professor of International Law at Rutgers University. He is the President of the Institute for World Order and the Director of the Institute's World Order Models Project.

# Global Political Alternatives

# 10

## Saul Mendlovitz

I decided to give this little session a title in order to give myself sufficient foolhardiness, if not courage, to present it to you. In this naming process I now have come up with three titles. The first is "The Citizenship and Politics of Planetary Humanism," and you can tell from the groans that's a no-no for this kind of group. The second title is "Governance in the Planetary Culture," a little better but still way off the mark, and the third one, which I think you'll agree with, is "The Boy with the Finger in the Dike." I hope to talk about the first two, but I'm likely to be talking about the third.

I would like to consider four categories in this discussion of citizenship, politics and governance in the planetary culture. The first is what I will call the sociology of this conference. The second I will call, in somewhat pretentious terms, the sociology of knowledge of the world order perspective and of the Institute for World Order. The third, some preferred world models, and the fourth, some transition proposals, deal with the actual work of the Institute.

In looking at the sociology of the conference, I begin with a statement which is obvious to all of you: thus far, the speakers have been male, white, over forty and graduates with Ph.D.'s or the functional equivalent from Western universities. There are no blacks; there are no Third Worlders. That comment is generally made in a snide way to criticize the conference and the people who organized it. But that is not what I intend to do, because if you invited the blacks and the Third Worlders they probably wouldn't come. They don't want to be here; it's not their thing. They feel they would be better off if left alone so that they might achieve their own dignity. In some sense, the absence of these people, despite the fact that I spend most of my life trying to involve myself with them, shouldn't be seen as negative; perhaps we should make a virtue of it by trying to understand what, if any, relationship we might usefully have with them.

*We should begin by talking about global culture with a special feeling for it, because we have helped create it by taking Scotch whiskey and the Beatles and Bach wherever we have gone*

Next, I would say that most of the people in this room are college trained and also that most have travelled outside the continental U.S.A. I would therefore make the point that we are a portion of the privileged class of the global community. So part of the sociology of this conference is that we are global citizens already. Citizenship implies responsibility—I want to talk about the kind of responsibility that it imposes upon us. It seems to me that we should begin by talking about global culture with a special feeling for it, because we have not only experienced it but have helped create it by taking Scotch whiskey and the Beatles and Bach wherever we have gone. (Christ knows what else we have taken wherever we have gone.)

Instead of criticizing the conference, I find a good deal to be said for it in personal terms. I find that the people I have been meeting here turn out to be my Third World and Fourth World. I have spent a good deal of my time in the last ten years running around the globe and meeting people in academic communities and in some policy elites. By and large, they are like me —they have gone through Western universities, they know all the rhetoric, they drink the same liquours, they have the same heroes and villains. So meeting with the people here who are establishing some new lifestyle through intentioned communities is, for me, meeting a kind of Third World in my own society. I very rarely meet such people abroad.

That moves me to my second topic, the sociology of knowledge of the world order perspective and of the Institute for World Order, which I will introduce by talking a little bit about how the Institute got started, what we thought we were about and why we are now here. The Institute for World Order, a research-educational foundation, was organized in the early 1960's by Harry and Betsy Hollins in conjunction with Grenville Clark. They were animated by the view, as I was when I joined them six months later, that it was possible to eliminate war as a human institution. That is to say, we took seriously, in the way the abolitionists must have done with the institution of slavery, the idea that we might be able to eliminate large-scale, organized violence if the appropriate strategy was brought to bear on that problem. The organization also had another vision, a model for a limited world government which we call world federalism. Clark, through his books (**A Plan for Peace,** 1951, and **World Peace Through World Law,** 1956, co-authored by Louis Sohn of Harvard) and through personal visits and letters, had been attempting to engage the political elite and moral authority figures throughout the globe in the notion that it was possible to transform the present system of militaristic, unilateral decision-making on the part of nation-states into some world federalist system in which war would be eliminated and there would be global institutions to handle claims, grievances, conflicts and the redistribution of income. In 1960, Clark was told by his doctor that he had a form of cancer, so he called upon the Hollinses to discuss how they might carry on his educational work. Together they came to the following conclusions:

*We took seriously, in the way the abolitionists must have done with slavery, the idea that we might be able to eliminate large-scale, organized violence*

1) The present policy elite throughout the globe, like most of the citizens of the world, operated within the paradigm of the nation-state system.

2) The nation-state system seemed to be moving in a self-destructive, or at least irreparably harmful, fashion.

3) There was no considerable pressure group for breaking that system.

4) A strategy was needed for breaking through.

Based on these conclusions, Clark and the Hollinses decided that if the policy elite could not be educated, then pressure groups should be established within societies to demand the kind of bold leadership that will be necessary for drastic system change. So they organized the Institute for World Order and embarked on a world-wide educational project to address the issues involved in system change—with the one important stipulation that a vision must be provided of what that new system would be if we got there. As part of this project, adult education groups were to be established all over the world to seriously consider these ideas. And I, just back from a visiting year with Louis Sohn at Harvard, became involved with the Institute as a teacher of one of those adult education courses.

We decided that we needed a ten year period to infiltrate the academic establishments of the globe with what we then called "war prevention" as a discipline, one that would meet academic standards and would supplant the traditional disciplines of international relations, international organization and comparative law. We made the decision to work within existing institutions. We did not expect to change those institutions in a profound structural way; we weren't going to de-school, we weren't even going to change the notion of a set curriculum. But we were going to change the substantive way people looked at problems. So we put together a set of course materials based on **World Peace Through World Law** and began introducing them into universities; we soon became part of what is now known as the Peace Studies Movement. Today in the United States there are a minimum of four hundred colleges that offer Peace Studies Programs. We are also in the process of establishing some ten world order centers.

Here I want to get into methodology and into why we moved from the term "war prevention" to the term "world order." Knowing that the enterprise we were engaged in was political and knowing that what we had to do was to change not only the minds of people in the United States but of significant numbers of people throughout the world, we began travelling, in 1962, to various parts of the globe to find out what was happening in other academic institutions concerning these problems. We discovered, as in the United States, that there were few places offering formal academic subjects on the matter but that there was a great deal of latent interest in it. We felt that if the appropriate instructional materials could be assembled we might be able to do something, so we began trying to identify and recruit people for our problem. In the process of learning and teaching we held a number of seminars in Third World countries. At one in Dar es Salaam in 1966 we discovered that some 50 percent of the participants were unwilling to read our materials, because members of the U.S. group were considered to be either straight-out CIA agents or dupes carrying out the old imperialism under a guise that we ourselves did not understand. In thinking about that, we decided that if the Third Worlders were encouraged to develop their own models of world order, their own models of war prevention, maybe they would act differently. We felt that if we asked groups of scholars in various parts of the world to produce their own constitutional models of world order and then put these different models together, we might have, if not the **Federalist Papers,** at least the **Pre-Federalist Papers** for the governance of a global community. The books are scheduled to come out in January through July of 1975.*

When we first went to these scholars, we said we were interested in their assistance in working on war prevention. While the Western Europeans and the Soviets understood what we were talking about, the people in Africa and Latin America and India said, ''Nonsense, that's not our problem. We understand it on one level as our problem, but our real problems are poverty and injustice. Now if you want to talk about poverty and injustice, we'll talk about war.'' So we began, for two reasons, to think of ourselves as dealing with poverty, war and injustice, rather than just war. One was a compelling ethical reason; obviously you want to help people who are in those straits. Secondly, there is the causal connectedness; most of the major wars of the world come out of the fact that there is poverty and injustice. After considering what perspective we would use, we decided to try to create, by sometime in the 1990s, a system in which those three problems would be handled in some acceptable minimal way for people throughout the globe. We picked this time frame because, first of all, we had a diagnostic view that we did not have more than ten to twenty years to avoid the catastrophes that were threatening us. Secondly, by picking the decade of the 1990s and by selecting people who are now around forty, we thought that we were taking ourselves out of the emotional and intellectual difficulties of the present problems, but that we were not putting ourselves so far down the line that we would not be held responsible for our recommendations. The methodology then became

*Preferred Worlds for the 1990s, Saul H. Mendlovitz, General Editor, a series published by The Free Press, New York, N.Y.

quite simple. We asked each group to make a diagnostic, prognostic statement for that time period and then to suggest a range of relevant utopias, specifying which of these was its preferred world, the world it really wanted. By relevant we meant that the transition process from the present system to that new system should be proposed.

Now I move into the topic of preferred worlds. To say that something is a social problem means that you have a value in your head, a normative statement about the way things ought to be. So in defining war, social injustice and poverty as problems, we had as values peace, social justice and economic well-being. (By economic well-being I mean the legal right for minimal subsistence.) One of the things we try to do is concretize and incarnate what we mean by these three values, so that people in our movement have targets to shoot for and so that we know where we are at each part of the journey. You like to know whether you're getting there or not. This, then, is the point I want to make about preferred worlds—you should get pretty concrete and behavioral about your goals. So I feel very strongly that one of the things a Lindisfarne or a New Alchemy can do is show us alternative lifestyles, incarnate models of a vision of the world we might want to live in. We must have some particular visions.

*I consider law to be a process of value realizing. My sense is that the notion of community is impossible without the notion of law*

As we go into the preferred world discussion, I want to introduce another kind of tension or dialectic. We have been discussing the centralization-decentralization problem and the problems of politics and culture. I would like to talk a little bit about law and community. I've been discussing the distribution of values in some equitable fashion. That's what I consider governance to be, and that's what I consider law to be; that is, law is a process of value realizing. My sense is that the notion of community is impossible without the notion of law. I cannot conceive of a community that does not have a governance structure that determines how the values in that community will be allocated and that resolves arguments about how they will be allocated. I argue that there is very little justice in a community without some constitutive order to handle grievances among people. We need the appropriate law within the appropriate community, and that's what I want to talk about in terms of the preferred worlds.

Although the Institute has now collected eight alternative models of preferred worlds from all over the globe, I will confine myself to the four discussed by Dick Falk in his book **A Study of Future Worlds.** The first is the federalist model of **World Peace Through World Law;** the second is the Nixon-Kissinger model, or what I call the concert of the globe model; the third is the Trilateral Commission or the multinational corporation model; and the fourth is something we call the populist model.

Now the world government or the world federalist model argues that if large-scale, organized violence is to be eliminated, then the nation-states must be disarmed and their capacities to re-arm must be limited. To do that, a system in which some sense of security is provided for the different participants is required. So world law, backed up by a legal regime and a world police force that could really tell heads of state not to build another weapon because it was against the law, is needed. If it were introduced, that kind of law—based on holding individuals responsible for derelictions and on not permitting them to hide behind the notion of acts of state—would radically change the system and establish a new normative order. A world court with compulsory jurisdiction of some kind is also required. This particular model, developed by Clark and Sohn, was very much concerned about the economic well-being of the rest of the globe and proposed a tax on the developed states of the world for development at the global level. So that is one model of world order: complete and general disarmament, centralized peacekeeping, compulsory jurisdiction and a global taxing agency. There is much to discuss about it both in terms of its Frankensteinian possibilities and its political feasibility.

The second model, the concert of the globe, is rapidly taking shape. That's Kissinger running around and making sure that Peking and Moscow are open even though we've bombed Haiphong and Hanoi. The important thing is to establish a relationship among the big powers of the world so that they understand that, while there may be some intense ideological conflicts, they will never go to war among each other—though perhaps they will use proxy clients to do that. There are two global problems the major powers must face, the spread of nuclear weapons and the ecological crisis. (Ecological stability, though I did not mention it, has become the fourth value of the world order perspective. There are some kinds of commodities that are desperately needed and will probably have to be shared.) The essence of this model is that the major powers will formally and informally deal with survival problems and more or less compete on other issues.

The third model, the Brzezinski or Trilateral Commission or multinational corporation model, arises out of a sense of the Trilateral Commission that central guidance, or world governance, is too important to leave to the governments of the world. Somehow or other, the thoughtful and responsible and prominent managerial elite has to be brought into it. The Trilateral Commission was set up to bring people from the OECD countries together to discuss ways to establish a global governance in which there would be a world without borders. Then the multinational corporation could go on producing and distributing goods the way it always has. The fight between this model and the previous model seems to me to be a kind of intramural fight among those who are already running the present system.

The fourth model is that of a populist governance for the globe. Here the idea of decentralization does make a great deal of sense. I was thinking, as John Todd was talking last night, about what would happen if every child was schooled to understand solar and wind energy and the fish farming cycle so that she or he would be able to set up a small, personal energy and food-producing system. If we did not have to rely upon the large-scale food production and distribution system because food was available within our own groups, that would change the way we govern. As another step in this model, we should move away from the notion of the nation-state system and develop the notion that humanity as a whole is the juridical unit. We should not ask how the nation-state system is working, but rather what the global problems are.

Let me give you three slogans before I move on to the next topic. If I think of what is needed in the area of armed security forces, my slogan is, "Let us move away from military to police." If I look at the ecological and economic well-being problems, I say, "Let's move from growth to need." And if I think of social injustice, I think, "Let's move from indignity and brutality to civility."

I now move to my last major category, some transition

proposals for the next five or ten years. Although we might not agree upon a particular preferred world, it is likely that we do have a sense of value sharing, which we need to incarnate in particular political projects. I would argue that if we do have some vague sense of what a preferred world would be, then we do need a series of transition steps. I've tried to develop some such steps, which should meet at least one of the following criteria:

1) The proposal should be based on the notion of benefit for all of humanity; that is, it should apply to global culture and global governance.

2) The proposal should highlight the inadequacies of the present operation of the existing nation-state system.

3) The proposal should lead to drastic system change rather than merely to a reformation of the present system, although there is a good deal to be said for the little boy putting his finger in the dike. It may be that he's got the exact point where he's holding the whole thing up and will give us some time to merely reform the system.

4) The proposal should have a political feasibility at what I would specify as the 5 to 20 percent level. Any proposal that has an 80 to 100 percent feasibility of coming into being is uninteresting because it's unlikely to change the system. On the other hand, anything under 5 percent and you begin to feel like a fool.

I want to argue that in the transition process an aggregation of proposals is needed. Each one of us may work on only one, but a common strategy is needed to aggregate a critical mass. Otherwise, the proposals will be co-opted into the current system and will not lead to drastic change. So I offer these projects to be done "all together, right now," as the song goes.

My first proposal is for the establishment of a standing, centralized peacekeeping force prepared to assume responsibility not only for border patrolling, as in the Middle East, but for humanitarian intervention. The incidences of large-scale, organized violence since World War II have all occurred in the Third World, and, with the exception of the United States' intervention in Korea and Vietnam, they have almost all been between brown and black people. The casualties add up to an incredible number of people. And in all these circumstances the global community sat by because of some kind of crazy notion that we call "domestic jurisdiction"; it refused to intervene within the domestic jurisdiction of a state. This is an insanity. It's a moral insanity to let those people fight and rape and pillage and loot each other that way because of some kind of notion. So I would argue for humanitarian intervention under very confined rules.

I think such intervention should start with the problem of apartheid in South Africa. It seems to me that a state which has a policy of practicing discrimination based on race is just so out of step with the normative ethic of the global culture that we can call it an outlaw nation. The people who run that state are technically criminals; they are committing crimes against humanity. It is permissible then, in fact it is obligatory, that the world community pick those individuals up, try them and establish a new regime. We frequently think of law and order as quelling somehow the underprivileged and those who are bringing about the good, but the fact is that we might use a centralized peacekeeping force to establish the dignity of humankind. That's how law and order might be used, and that's how I see the relationship between peacekeeping and social justice.

My second proposal is for the establishment of a comprehensive ocean regime for the benefit of all humanity. The traditional doctrine of sea law has been freedom of the seas, which meant that the sea belonged to no one. Elizabeth Borghese and her group have begun to argue at the U.N. and elsewhere that, since the ocean belongs to no one, the better way to phrase it is that the ocean belongs to everyone. If it belongs to everyone then it has to be used for the betterment of everyone. This means you have to establish a regime which insures that. The Law of the Sea conferences are a small, preliminary step in that direction.

My third transition proposal is that teeth be given to the U.N. Environment Agency. How do you start creating some implementation machinery?

A fourth proposal is for an agency I think we need desperately, a global food agency. We need, as a minimum, a monitoring agency and some kind of food banks. We also ought to establish the right to food as a legal right, and people all over the globe should have a place where they can go and enforce that right by a writ or some legal thing. Whether we then have to move to some global system of socialist productivity is something I haven't made up my mind about. I'm now impressed by the possibility of decentralization of food production that John Todd has suggested.

I also argue that we need the beginnings of some genuine world tax scheme. Here I go to the Russian academician Sakharov, who in his 1967 document "Freedom, Co-Existence and Progress" argued that the developed areas of the world should give 20 percent of their gross national income for a twenty year period to the Third World. That such an idea came from the Soviet Union in such a blatant form—it was suggested as a matter of right—is an incredible thing. If we establish a global political system in which all people are entitled to live just as we are entitled to live, then maybe we can have something to say about their population explosions.

Now these are the kinds of transition proposals that I think we should be engaged in. They do not yet talk about the actual political process. I haven't any specific transition process, but it does seem to me that the educative process we are all involved in, the consciousness raising, should be built around these issues. I'm not arguing against the kind of cultural transformation that comes out of spirituality and renaissance and consciousness of one another, but I am arguing that we need to become sufficiently expert in these global issues so that we can provide political pressure. We keep saying that we don't want to give things over to the experts and the technocrats. Well, if we don't, we had better do it ourselves. Somehow, we have got to do it.

So I would argue for the educative process and for plain old political pressure. That's very mundane; it's back to the political process. I wish there was some other way. I wish that somehow we could confront these on-going problems with some other form of social movement. I do not deny the necessity for the myth, for the infusion of the spirit. But we also have the responsibility of relating to and, perhaps, actively participating in a political process which will promote a humanist-populist community.

Jonas Salk, developer of the polio vaccine that bears his name, is a Fellow of the Salk Institute for Biological Studies in La Jolla, California. He is the author of Man Unfolding and The Survival of the Wisest.

# The Consciousness of Evolution

# 11

## *Jonas Salk*

I would like to speak about consciousness of evolution, about the evolution of consciousness, and about the dialectical process involved in both.

Each of us sees things differently. Though we have different backgrounds and use different sets of images and metaphors, we are all sensitive to the current crises and dangers in the world. Each of us is a kind of instrument of the evolutionary process—is capable of questioning whether our future evolution can be influenced consciously.

The human individual, produced in the course of evolution, possesses a mind with the capacity to perceive itself. I experience a sense of wonder when I think of humans as having evolved from physical matter to living matter to the point where "human matter" is capable of perceiving itself.

For consciousness to be useful, we must learn to see ourselves as we really are, as well as how we would like to be. In order to do so, we need to see the familiar from an unfamiliar viewpoint. We need to see that the various forces that impel us are all aspects of the same unity, as are life and death, desire and fear, expressing and coping, acting as tools and weapons. This is also reflected in the Chinese ideogram for "crisis" which is made up of two symbols—one meaning danger and the other opportunity. The use of the word "crisis," therefore, evokes the idea and feeling both of "danger" and of "opportunity." The meaning given to it by the individual mind will depend upon the context in which the word is used as well as upon the attitude of the mind, whether positive or negative. Thus, attitude will determine whether an individual's response to "crisis" will be optimistic or pessimistic.

Through awareness and consciousness it is conceivable that we could influence the future course of events, qualitatively or quantitatively. However, because of the influence of Nature, humans alone cannot determine the future. When we attempt to control evolution, we see the narrow realm within which we have free will; we become aware of the existence of an inexorable force—the evolutionary process—which, if tampered with, often bites back. We are speaking, therefore, about a dangerous game. We should explore the limits within which we do have freedom. We may find that realm very narrow indeed.

I share Gregory Bateson's concern about the difficulty of recognizing the consequences of all that we do when we introduce a change. I acknowledge the enormous dangers. The Rockefeller Foundation, for example, with its humanitarian impulse and great beneficence, caused malaria to be eliminated in the Mauritius Islands, reducing infant and child mortality from this disease. The consequences in terms of the population explosion and the misery that followed are well known. Similarly, we are altering the human gene pool through acting out our humanitarian impulses. At some point, we will have to re-examine our values and priorities and begin to look at ourselves from an evolutionary viewpoint. We are at a moment of crisis—of danger **and** opportunity. How do we conduct ourselves at such a moment? Can we consciously move into the future and influence our destiny favorably?

It is possible to see evolution in man's relationships, values and attitudes from competition to coexistence to cooperation, from help for subsistence to help for self-sufficiency, from independence to interdependence. In the history of man, having valued individual survival, we are now conscious of the need to value species survival. In the past, territorial respect dominated; hopefully, in the future, human respect will dominate.

In the interrelationship between sets of related forces, as the cooperative **both/and attitude** increases, the competitive **either/or attitude** diminishes. This is a way of seeing how the process of evolution proceeds, not only through the disappearance of something that previously existed, but through the appearance of something new. Whatever new is introduced, either a positive or a negative effect will occur. Not all changes will necessarily be advantageous. However, the evolutionary process advances on the basis of selection of that which is advantageous. This provides at least a measure of hope, as we examine alternatives to the dire consequences predicted by some.

Environment is one of the multiplicity of factors that affect evolution and development. If we are to use consciousness for evolution, we must be conscious both of complexity and of order in the interrelationship of man and environment. Humans who are the producers of human culure, including science and technology, have an effect on the physical environment and on the biological environment. The opposite is also true.

In comparing scientists, we can, by their orientation, distinguish three groups—naturalists, experimentalists and theoreticians. Naturalists, engaged in explanatory science, tell how things are built; experimentalists, engaged in predictive science, tell how things work; and theoreticians, engaged in anticipatory science, tell how things might be improved. We have reached a stage where theoretical projections into the future can now be enriched by the epistemologic contributions of the experimentalists and the naturalists—making the questions posed valid, reasonable, and discussable.

Science is built fundamentally by the development of knowledge in an ordered way. **Science for science's sake** is an attempt to discern the nature of order. **Science for man** is concerned with the application of that knowledge for improving the human condition, or the quality of life. Mathematics, for example, is developed for its own sake and is also applied to practical problems in physics. The principles of physics are applied to further understanding the nature of order in the physical realm. Physics is studied for its own sake and can also be applied to chemistry, biology, or physiology, each of which can also be studied for itself as well as for its application to solving human problems. There is a kind of evolutionary force which impels this process of increasing understanding along a path from the simple to the more complex.

When we use the word "evolution" and the word "growth" as an expression of the evolutionary force, we imply that order exists. One expression of order is the formula, $E = mc^2$. The presence of this law, and others of a similar nature, indicates that the evolutionary process began with the manifestation of the existence of such laws and suggests the "existence" of order in a non-manifest form. Just as we accept the existence of order in the physical and biological realms, scientific minds are now attempting to discern the nature of order in the realm of the mind—a subject that until recently few persons with a background in science were willing to speak of or to think about. Why has this change taken place? Perhaps it is because we have reached a point in evolution where we can now draw upon the epistemological contributions of scientists who have until now been studying the nature of order in the physico-chemical and biological realms, and the evolutionary process has resulted in the development of an order of complexity whereby the human mind can now study itself.

I keep looking for a way to illustrate* what I am trying to say about **consciousness of evolution** and of **unity and diversity.** If we start with an example from biology, we see that the unit is comprised of the **genotype-phenotype,** or what I call the **gene-soma** dualism. The gene contains the information for making proteins (soma) which, in turn, are essential for making the genetic material (gene). Similarly, the species is comprised of individuals, and without individuals there would be no species. Thus, the sociobiological unit is also made up of two components.

*The Survival of the Wisest, Jonas Salk, 1973, Harper & Row, New York, N.Y.

A similar duality is seen in the chemical atom which consists of protons and electrons. In the physical realm, the unity/duality pattern is also seen in the energy-mass relationship. The metabiological unit—the level of mind which is manifest in creation and transcendence—consists of **being** and **ego**. These terms and this concept are elaborated elsewhere.*

Humankind is, in a sense, coming of age, and its humanness should now have an opportunity to emerge. For the past ten thousand years or so, the possibility of conscious evolution has been developing; we have been in the process of preparing for what can happen now. We are between two epochs* which I call Epoch A and Epoch B. The predominant attitude will in time shift from anti-disease to pro-health, from death control to birth control, from self-repression to self-expression. External restraints of the past are now, in some cultures, demanding replacement by self-restraint. This may be seen as a natural evolutionary phenomenon.

The great conflicts among opposing elements from the past coexisting in today's culture bring about crises which pose **opportunities as well as dangers.** There is a tendency for some individuals to want to keep things unchanged, with the effect that the dialectic process tends to maintain oscillation about a mean. Evolution has been in process for a long time, and we are now at a point where, in the human realm, it is proceeding even more rapidly because of explosive expansion of the culture of science and technology, which I see as a product of human metabiological activity.

*For the past ten thousand years or so, the possibility of conscious evolution has been developing; we have been preparing for what can happen now*

Intraspecies conflicts among humans seem to be more metabiological than biological. Such conflicts as between ego and being, intellect and intuition, reason and feeling can be resolved not in terms of **either/or** but as **both/and.** The elements of these pairs, as time goes on, should not be separated and alienated from each other but should function together. Are we capable of dealing with the evolutionary process in such a way that this fusion can occur? We need a philosophy based on both/and rather than on either/or, on unity and complementarity instead of duality and dichotomy. We must reconcile such concepts as present and future, quantity and quality, extremes and balance, parts and whole.

*Ibid.

The kind of change with which we are being confronted is of a magnitude analogous to the difference in perception brought about by the discovery that the earth was round, not flat. Now we are dealing not with a perceptual difference alone but with an actual difference in the change between Epoch A and Epoch B and in the change in relationships in the human realm which this evokes.

Our consciousness of nature and our consciousness of ourselves are both increasing, so that now we are conscious of evolution and are also witnessing evolution of our consciousness. Consciousness of evolution and evolution of consciousness cause us to question the degrees of freedom we have for conscious evolution.

Since the birth of the sun, evolution has been leading to this critical point in human evolution and in the evolution of humankind. We are alive at this important juncture when we can be conscious of all this, able to ponder such questions and possibly even able to contribute consciously, in some measure, to the future of human evolution.

Gregory Bateson has been a seminal influence in many fields—biology, ethnology, linguistics, psychotherapy, epistemology. He developed the ''Double Bind'' theory of schizophrenia and participated in the Macy Foundation conferences that founded the science of cybernetics. His book Steps to an Ecology of Mind is a collection of his essays written over a period of forty years. Most of all, Gregory is a teacher. Currently he is on the Board of Regents of the University of California and teaches at UC Santa Cruz.

# 12 The Thing of It Is

## Gregory Bateson

The thing of it is that these are very difficult things to talk about because there are three aspects of the matter which people think are different problems, different concerns, which in fact boil down to being all one matter. I put these three up on the board. One of them is **evolutionary theory,** and that is a matter, you know, which is dealt with in one sort of book. Another is **mind-body problems,** and that is dealt with in another sort of book, and the third is **epistemology,** and that is dealt with again in another sort of book.

I want to get across to you that these three apparently different matters are in fact all one subject of discourse and that you cannot handle one without simultaneously handling the others. If we are going to talk about "consciousness," I would like to aim that word specifically at an awareness of these three things and their interrelations.

Let us start from where we were last night. We had a lot of Cartesian diagrams in which time was horizontal and responsibility or narcissism or something or other was the vertical coordinate. These diagrams were on the model of what Descartes thought was the way to think—a model which has been extraordinarily profitable in thinking about a lot of things like planets and temperatures and even perhaps populations. (I'm not too sure about populations.) The model is, at any rate, fashionable still among those who study populations.

Now, it's not an accident that the man who designed those graphs was the man who also formalized the dualism between mind and matter. And it's very curious that this should be so. I want to get across to you that when you do this—when you start arranging your words and explanations on that sort of a tautology, that set of basic notions about how things are related—you will of necessity end up with the sort of split between mind and body that Descartes ended up with. That split, you know, has been the battleground of science, especially of biology, for a very long time. And the problem is how to get away from it.

You see, the moment you go to the extreme materialistic end, which has these dimensions and quantities in it, and the nice curves and all the rest of it, the moment you specialize on that side, the thing bubbles up on the mental side with all sorts of mental-spiritual notions which you excluded from your materialism. You squeezed them out from one context and they bubbled up in another. The moment you do that, you're split wide open.

Now, it may be that there are total splits in the universe. I prefer to believe that it is rather one universe than two, but the only real argument for that, you know, is Occam's razor; it's less trouble to believe in one universe than to believe in two. It's miraculous enough that there be one. Believe me.

There is also, you see, a consciousness of how it is to think, how it is to engage in trial and error and so on, and that consciousness, as far as I can make out, is roughly called **prajna** in Tibetan Buddhism. It's a useful word if that's what it means. (It's always difficult to be sure with Sanscrit.) So what do we do?

There's a very curious theorem called Euler's theorem. You remember at school you were taught you should not add apples and miles. And that was a very useful thing to learn. It's very useful in reading equations to sort out the syntax of the dimensions. If you have $E = mc^2$, you have to remember that m is of the dimension of mass (not matter but mass); c is of the dimension of length divided by time—it's a velocity. So $c^2$ is length squared divided by time squared. E therefore is of the dimension of mass times the square of a length divided by the square of a time, and that's all E is, you know. A **quantity,** of those dimensions.

Now, Euler's theorem in topology says that in any polyhedron—that's a solid, three-dimensional figure with edges and faces and apices where the edges meet—that the number of faces plus the number of apices equals the number of edges plus two. Let me do that on the blackboard.

$$\text{Faces + apices = edges + 2}$$

There's a horrid question, you see: what is the dimension of the number "2"? We have been grossly adding surfaces to meeting points and then equating them with edges, and then there's this "2." We appear to have mixed our dimensions hopelessly. What is the solution to this difficulty?

The theorem stands. It is probably the "fundamental" theorem of topology. How then is it right that these quantities should be added in this funny way? And what is the dimension of two? I made a crack on the side last night, asking Jonas whether he was sure that the subject matter we are dealing with is a subject matter within which the concept of dimensions, and therefore quantities and graphs and all the rest, is appropriate. Is this an appropriate language for talking about such matters at all? I sort of let that pass as a wisecrack last night, but now we have to face it more seriously.

You see, that fellow in the boat there thinks he is going at a "speed." He thinks he can measure the speed with a speedometer. But that's really not true in psychology. The truth is that he's having fun. And the relationship of the fun to the speed is very obscure. Perhaps what he's having fun with is (his opinion about) the **probability** of disaster. Probabilities, you know, are of zero dimensions. I don't know the dimensions of "opinion."

You see, we've been pulling these analogies and metaphors out of physics and then trying to map human behavior, love, hate, beauty, ugliness onto those metaphors.

God, language is a lousy invention, isn't it?

**Question:** Are you sure it's a dimension?

**Bateson:** Language? I'm sure that it is not a dimension. I am sure that the epistemology for forms and patterns is different from the implicit epistemology of hard science. We have **names** of faces, **names** of edges, **names** of apices, and that's what we're playing with. Not "faces," "edges" and "apices." And because the whole thing is removed to a higher level of abstraction, in a curious way it becomes legitimate to add them together and subtract them and all the rest of it. Euler's theorem is in the Platonic universe, in the universe of ideas, and not in the universe of dimensions. In this Platonic universe, the analogues of dimensions are names and classes and logical types. We are dealing not with "real" dimensions but with descriptions of dimensions, and the big enlightenment comes when you suddenly realize that all this stuff is **description**. And when you realize that, then you realize that it's possible to be wrong in how you **organize** your descriptions, and it's possible to be wrong for this reason: the creatures we talk about—people, sea urchins, starfish, beetles, plants, cabbages, whatnot—all these creatures themselves contain description. The DNA are descriptive prescriptions, injunctions,

*The big enlightenment comes when you suddenly realize that all this stuff is description*

for how to make a bird or a man or whatever. And these injunctions, therefore, themselves contain epistemology. They contain an implicit theory of the nature of description. You can never get away from theories of the nature of description whenever, wherever you have descriptions. All descriptions are based on theories of how to make descriptions. You cannot claim to have no epistemology. Those who so claim have nothing but a bad epistemology. And every description is based upon, and contains implicitly, a theory of how to describe. The Cartesian coordinates contain a theory of how to describe, and for many purposes, I believe, it is an inappropriate and dangerous theory—one which in the end leads to various sorts of quantification of "things" which probably should be regarded as patterns, not quantities. It also leads to conceptual separation of mind from matter. You see, you can be wrong in describing the anatomy of a human being when you say he has five banana-like objects on the end of each limb, because, you see, he might not have "five fingers" on the end of each limb, but "four angles between fingers." The question is, what is there in the genetic injunctions, the prescriptive descriptions, for how to make a hand? Is there a number at all? "Five," or "four," or whatever? Is there conceivably a rule of symmetry there? Is each limb itself primarily bilaterally symmetrical, like a feather? We have here an almost total gap in our genetic knowledge.

*You cannot claim to have no epistemology. Those who so claim have nothing but a bad epistemology*

There are few little spots in genetics where there are indications of what the epistemology, what the theory of prescription might be. Let me give you a couple of cases because I want now to start thinking in terms of biological systems or universes which are organized by information, i.e., by significant **differences** rather than by forces or impacts.

Vertebrates and chordates are, on the whole, bilaterally symmetrical in their ectoderm and mesoderm. The endoderm is always profoundly asymmetrical. There are a few cases of asymmetry, and fairly superficial asymmetry, in ectoderm and mesoderm (in owls and cetaceans). Why the endoderm is more asymmetrical than the rest, Lord alone knows. So we ask, where does the bilateral symmetry come from? Not the genes. Oh no. It's doubtful whether the DNA and genes could ever be able to tell the embryo how to orient itself. An unfertilized frog's egg (and this has been known since the 20's and presumably this goes

Gregory Bateson 147

Frog's Egg ..

Plane of symmetry / Animal pole

Entry point of spermatozoon

Vegetal pole.

for all vertebrates) is, so far as we know, radially symmetrical. It has a differentiated north pole and a south pole but is the same all around the equator. It's pigmented down to rather below the equator. This top ("animal") end is fairly clear of fat, while the other ("vegetal") end is heavily fat. The egg is sort of yellow down here and nearly black on the top. But it's the same all the way around, so far as we know. The nucleus is located somewhere near the top. Now, how will the egg decide on the line of bilateral symmetry, the plane of bilateral symmetry?

The answer is that a spermatozoon will enter somewhere below the equator. That defines three points—two poles and the point of entry—and that line of longitude, that meridian, will be the middle line of the embryo. You don't have to have a spermatozoon; you can do it with a fiber of a camel's hair brush. Just prick it and the egg will develop and will make a complete frog which will be haploid. It will only have half the number of chromosomes it should have and will be sterile, but it will catch flies and hop like any proper frog. All the information for catching flies and hopping is there.

This experiment tells us something of what the genetic code looks like. The genetic code—the unfertilized egg—has sufficient information to pose a **question**. It can set the egg to a readiness to receive a piece of information. But the genetic code does not contain the answer to that question. It must wait for something outside the egg, a spermatozoon or a camel's hair fiber, to fix it. This, you see, sets a whole stage for asking, **what is the unit of embryology?** And the unit is not just that egg; the unit is the egg **plus** the answer. And without the egg plus the answer, you cannot go on to the next phase. And so on.

148        Evolution and the Strategies of Consciousness

Let me now give you another piece of experimental data about the nature of this whole business. We take a newt embryo, and I will draw it in profile, facing to the right. At a certain point a low mountain starts to swell up, and that swelling is the limb bud of the right fore limb. And remember that this limb is different from the left limb and that that difference couldn't be in the DNA, because the same DNA are in the cells on the right side that are in the cells on the left. So where does the difference come from?

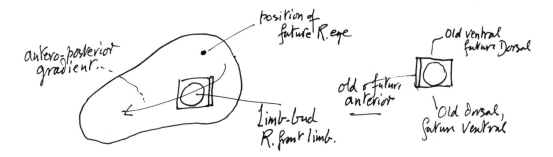

Anyway, that is the limb bud for the right fore limb. Now we cut it out and lift it and turn it through 180 degrees and put it back in. The former front edge is now the back edge, and the old ventral edge is now the dorsal edge. And the old posterior now points forward. It'll grow in the new position, and when it grows what do you think? It grows into a **left** leg!

Why?

It grows into a left leg because it **knows**. It has received the information or injunction and is governed by the information. I'm not talking about consciousness, I'm talking about being determined by information. I do not know whether it's conscious. I'm not a limb bud of an anthropologist—of an amphibian.

It seems that the body of the embryo has a fore and aft gradient which was determined before it even developed a bulge which was the bud. Such gradients are informational gradients. Lord knows what they depend on—it could be clockwork for all I know. It doesn't matter, you see. Any **difference** could serve as information. It could be electrical, chemical, what have you.

That fixes the fore and aft differentiation in the bud. But the dorsal-ventral information comes much later. We did our operation before the bud knew the dorsal-ventral answers, which later it gets from its neighborhood. So now this edge is told to be a "dorsal" by the neighboring tissues; and the old dorsal edge is told to be a "ventral" by the neighbors. The ground plan for the limb is complete. It **must** come out this way. The proximal-distal dimension is unchanged; so the ground plan is that of a **left** leg. We have inverted one dimension (the dorsal-ventral) but not the other. If you invert one dimension of a three-dimensional object, as in a mirror, you get the inverted mirror image.

This world of morphogenesis obeys a topological logic. One-dimensional inversion gives you the mirror image, two inverted dimensions give you the ortho image again, and three dimensions give you the inverted image again. What I'm saying is that the world into which we are moving, the world in whose terms we have to think, is a world of patterns, and in that world there are tautologies and logics which we can use for explaining, for building accurate language and for creating some rigor. It's not like the language of quantities and such things. It's a language of patterns and, for most of us, an unfamiliar business.

We have a major problem in front of us to create the language in which we can talk about evolution, about morphogenesis, about epistemology and about mind-body.

We are going to deal with trial and error in these matters, and the old lineal and transitive logic that we were brought up with was devoid of time. There were some nice patterns in Euclid and elsewhere, but timeless: "If straight lines are defined in this way and points are defined in that way and triangles are defined so and so, and if two triangles have three sides of the one equal to three sides of the other, then the two triangles are equal, each to each." That's the way I learned it. But look at the word "then." There's no time in that "then." There is nothing but logic in it. Now, consider the sequence: "If a frog's egg receives a spermatozoon on a given meridian, **then** that meridian will define the plane of bilateral symmetry." That "then" has time in it. Sequential time. An effect follows always with a delay.

If Epimenides was right in saying that Cretans always lie, and he was a Cretan, was he a liar or not a liar? If he was a liar, **then** he was not a liar. If he was not a liar, **then** it was untrue that Cretans are always liars, and so on. Now, look at the "then" in that paradox. If yes, then no. If no, then yes. If the "then" is logical, there is paradox, but if the "then" is causal and temporal, the contradiction disappears. The sequence is like that of the electric bell on the front door. If the circuit is complete, then a magnet is activated which will break the circuit. If the circuit is broken, then the magnet will not be activated, and the circuit will be restored. If the circuit is restored, then the magnet will be activated, and the circuit will be broken, and so on. So we get an oscillation, and the paradox "if yes then no; if no then yes" contains a real **temporal** "then."

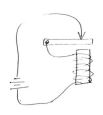

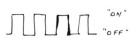

Such oscillating systems are operated by thresholds—not by states but by **differences** and changes and even differences between changes. There is information not only in our words but also in the processes which we describe. It's nice to have the explanation in step with the system of ideas within the process which you are explaining.

This is what I keep saying. If we are going to say that the thing has "five fingers," we may be wrong because really it has four gaps between fingers—four relationships between fingers, because growth is governed by relationships, not by the absolutes.

Now, if you are going to face oscillating systems, you meet a very curious circumstance—that a certain degree of **reality** is imparted to the "system," the chunk of living matter. There is a justification of some sort in drawing a line around it, perhaps giving it a name. That justification is based on the fact of autonomy, of literal "autonomy," in that the system names itself. The injunctions which govern the system necessarily are messages which **stand for** or name the system. The system is auto-self-nomic, self-naming or self-ruling. And that is the only autonomy there is, as far as I know. It's recursiveness, and recursiveness is crucial to any system containing **if-then** links, where the "then" is not a logical but a temporal "then."

*It's nice to have the explanation in step with the system of ideas within the process which you are explaining*

I'm now starting to build up, you see, slowly, to where we can begin to think. By introducing time into the if-then relations, we have made classical logic obsolete. But that doesn't mean, you know, that it is now impossible to think. It means that classical logic is a poor simulation of cause. We used to ask, "Can computers simulate logic?" But computers work on if-then relations that are causal: "If this transistor tickles that transistor,

**then** such-and-such.'' That's a causal ''if-then,'' with time in it.

The truth of the matter is that logic is a very poor simulation of computers and other causal systems. But this does not mean that there are not regularities, patterns and epistemologies; there are other ways of describing which are better representations of how to think. I keep coming back to the assertion that what we deal with are descriptions, second order **representations** of how it is. How it primarily is, we don't know. We can't get there. The **ding an sich** is always and inevitably out of reach. You have sense organs specially designed to keep the world out. It is like the lining of your gut, which is specially designed to keep out foreign proteins, to break down the foreign protein before it enters the blood stream. The protein must be broken down to amino acids. Only the amino acids are allowed through. Your sense organs similarly break down the information or ''news'' to the firing of end organs, which is another piece of this whole business. The mystery of epistemology is still how anything knows anything, how it is that an egg can be organized; and you're only eggs, and I'm only eggs, you know. We're the phenotypic try-out of eggs. The hen is the egg's way of finding out whether it was a good egg. If the hen's no good, the egg was lousy. It had the wrong genes or something. The system is all trial and error. That's not quite what Samuel Butler said, but pretty near it. He said the hen was the egg's way of making another egg. It's really the egg's way of finding out if it was any good in evolutionary terms.

So we face two levels of trial and error. There is the evolutionary testing of the phenotype, but also there is the thinking which happens inside the phenotype—another stochastic process with a shorter time span. The same sort of thinking has got to be used to analyze evolution as the thinking you use to analyze thought. Not that they're the same process. I do not believe that what you think can alter your ova or spermatozoa; I'm not preaching a Lamarckian message at all. Indeed, quite the contrary. I **am** saying that there is a non-quantitative and non-lineal way of thinking about things which is common to the evolutionary process and the process of thought. And therefore, epistemology and evolution go hand in hand. The problems of mind-body obviously are the same sort of business. And what you think about evolution is going to be the reflection of what you think about mind-body relations and what you think about thought. It's all going to move along together.

But thought processes and evolutionary processes are of different logical type. Never the twain shall meet. Let us examine for a moment the nature of purpose in individuals and in adaptive changes in phylogeny. Pragmatism. Wonderful.

But let us suppose that in biological evolution there is a direct communicational bond between individual experience which will induce somatic change, as it's called, and the DNA injunctions to be passed on to the next generation. Let us imagine for the moment a Lamarckian universe, in which, if I tan myself in the sun, this will in some degree be passed on as increased brownness of the skin of my offspring. In such a system, my offspring will have **lost** a flexibility. They will no longer have my freedom. By hypothesis, I am flexible. I go brown in the sun, or I go bleach with no sun. But Lamarckian theory would presume a rigidity in my offspring, a reduction of their ability to bleach with no sun. Obviously a Lamarckian theory will in the end enforce an increasing rigidity, a loss of the ability to adapt, and that won't do. Things are going to get too tight. Our description of the body is made up of a very large number of variables, which interlock in all sorts of rings and loops, so that if you start tightening on any one of them, you will **ipso facto** tighten others, ending up with no tolerance or flexibility anywhere. This happens with disease or even with a cold in the head. We put people in bed and keep them warm when they have a cold because they've lost a lot of flexibility by being stressed up to the maximum or minimum somewhere in their organization. We therefore protect them during that period.

*In social evolution there is no barrier corresponding to that between phenotype and genotype*

Evidently Lamarckian inheritance would present severe problems for biological evolution, and the barrier between somatic change and genetic change seems to be quite important. I said earlier that this barrier or contrast is really a contrast in logical typing, and this is important. The trouble is that I don't want my offspring to be more brown than I. I want them to be more able to turn brown. This will pay evolutionary dividends. But this is a change of different logical type from what Lamarckians envisage. In social evolution there is no barrier corresponding to that between phenotype and genotype. Consider the invention of carbon paper. This prevented the slavery depicted in Dickens' lawyers' offices where miserable people are copying documents. That was made largely obsolete by the invention of carbon paper. Fine, but within a few years of the invention of carbon paper, we started to use it for personal letters, even for love letters, because, after all, posthumously we'd like our biographers to have access to our most romantic thoughts. Today our filing cabinets are overfull. The adoption of any invention becomes irreversible very quickly. It becomes built deeply, irreversibly, into the physiology of our society within very few years of invention. There is no barrier between immediate adaptation and pickling the change into society.

For this reason, more than for any other, I distrust consciousness as a gimmick added to the evolutionary scene. Conscious cerebration is much too fast. It doesn't give any time for growth into the new state of affairs. There is no trial and error or tentative assimilation which would slowly flow, hesitate and flow, hesitate and flow, into new patterns.

*Is the adaptation one which we can really stand?*

If I were to try to **apply** my theories to the changing social scene, I think that that is where my pragmatic remarks would focus—not on the question of immediate adaptations, but on long term changes. I would want some sort of meta trial and error which would deal with the question, "Is the adaptation one which we can really stand?" This would give us some chance of adapting not just to the immediate problem of who dies of what or the traffic accidents or the minor discomforts of the suburbs. We might have time to ask: "If we make this adaptation in law, in technology, in whatever, to disease, to discomforts, to traffic accidents, what will be the implications of that adaptation to the rest of the system, which is all interlinked?" In the end, it is the meta-adaptation, the adaptation of the total adaptive system that is going to kill us or let us live.

155

*Lewis Thomas has been a Professor and Dean at New York University-Bellevue Medical Center and at Yale Medical School. In 1975 he won the National Book Award for* The Lives of *a Cell. Currently he is the President of the Memorial Sloan-Kettering Cancer Center in New York and a member of the National Academy of Sciences.*

# At the Mercy of Our Defenses?

# 13

## Lewis Thomas

It seems to me that any discussion of aspects of human consciousness ought to have room somewhere in it for the problems of disease and death. There are some fairly new things, I think, to say about each, which could have an influence on the way we begin to view them. And it does seem to me safe to predict that any new information which can alter our collective attitudes about disease and toward death might sooner or later have some effect on our collective consciousness.

I should say at the outset that I take a generally meliorist viewpoint. It seems to me that it's going to turn out that things are rather better for us than we have been accustomed in our despair to think. I bring up as illustrations several items about disease. There is a microorganism called the meningococcus—the cause of epidemic meningitis. Viewed from some distance it appears to have all the characteristics of an implacable, dangerous enemy of the whole human race. Epidemics sweep through military barracks and across schoolyards and sometimes over the populations of whole cities. The organism invades the bloodstream and then invades the meningeal space, or the coverings over the brain and spinal cord, and the outcome is meningitis — a formidable and, in the days before chemotherapy, a highly fatal affliction. And the engagement has the look of specificity in the sense that the meningococcus appears to be particularly adapted for life in the covering membranes of the brain and spinal cord of human beings. You might say that it makes its living this way, a predator with us as the prey.

But it is not so. When you compare the total number of people who are infected by the meningococcus to the number of people who come down with meningitis, the arrangement has a quite different look. Cases of actual meningitis are always a tiny minority. There is an infection of the majority, to be sure, but it is confined to the back of the throat and almost always goes unnoticed by the infected people; they produce antibodies against the meningococcus a few days after infection, and the organisms may or may not persist in the mucous membranes of the throat, but that's the end of the affair. There is no invasion of the central nervous system.

Cases of meningitis are the exception. The meningococcal infection, as a rule, is benign and transient — more like an equable association than an infection. It seems unlikely that the mysterious development of meningitis in some patients represents any special predilection of the bacteria. It may be that the defense mechanisms of affected patients are flawed in some special way we don't yet understand so that the meningococci are granted access, invited in, so to say. But whatever the cause, the disease is a sort of abnormal event in nature, rather like an accident.

There is a virus ubiquitous among mice called lymphocytic choriomeningitis virus, for short LCM. The classical disease is a lethal form of meningitis, in which the inflammation over the surface of the brain is composed entirely of lymphocytes — small mono-nucleated cells which are found both in the bloodstream and in the lymph nodes and are now known to be responsible in large part for all immunologic reactions. At first glance this disease of the mouse appears to represent an invasion of, and damage to, the central nervous system by a virus specifically adapted for this kind of behavior. But in actual fact the disease turns out to be caused by invasion of the brain surface by the host's own lymphocytes. This invasion, rather than any special neurotoxic property of the virus, produces death. If you prevent the lymphocyte response from occurring, and you can do this by producing an infection with LCM virus either late in the fetal life of mice or within the first day or so after the animals are born, then the mice become what is technically known as "tolerant" to the virus. The outcome is a persistent virus infection everywhere in the tissues of the animal, including the central nervous system, but with no evidence of central nervous system disease. Now if you have an animal that is tolerant and has virus circulating in all his tissues including the brain and you restore his immunologic reactivity to normal (and you can do so by transplanting into him lymph nodes or lymphocytes from normal mice of the same line), then the animal, after an incubation period of a few days, becomes ill with typical lymphocytic choriomeningitis. The new lymphocytes swarm over the surface of the brain, evidently looking for the virus. For reasons not understood, this reaction proves to be fatal. The disease is, essentially, the result of the host's response to the virus.

*The disease is, essentially, the result of the host's response to the virus*

Cortisone, which among its numerous other properties has the capacity to turn off various defense reactions against bacteria, also seems to turn off the most conspicuous clinical manifestations of infectious disease. In the early 1950's, soon after cortisone became available for clinical research, Max Finland of the Boston City Hospital treated several patients who had come in with classical pneumococcal lobar pneumonia. He observed what at first seemed to be a miraculous clinical cure. Within just a few hours after the first dose of cortisone the fever, malaise, prostration, chest pain, and even the cough typical of lobar pneumonia vanished. The patients insisted that they were entirely well, wanted to be allowed up and around the ward, and asked for dinner. According to the X-rays, however, the disease was making alarming progress and spreading to the lungs. The experiment was promptly terminated and never performed again. Subsequently, other investigators observed a similarly dramatic

Lewis Thomas    159

elimination of all subjective and objective disease manifestations in typhoid fever and in various forms of typhus fever. In each of these instances, however, the dramatic improvement and restoration of good health was associated with an altogether unacceptable trade-off—enhanced spread of the infection.

The most spectacular examples of host governance of disease mechanisms that I can think of are the array of responses that various animals, including man, make to what are called the endotoxins of gram negative bacteria. These endotoxins are the lipopolysaccharide materials present in the cell walls of a wide variety of gram negative bacteria, including the typhoid bacillus, bucelli, the cause of undulant fever, E. coli, and a number of others. The mystery here is that the microbial toxin which can kill out of hand any one of a very large number of animal species does not, when injected by vein, even seem in itself to be toxic. It does have a remarkable effect on a variety of the mechanisms which participate in the defense of the host. For example, the endotoxin has the capacity to enhance enormously the coagulability of blood; it also affects the cellular mechanisms responsible for making antibodies, the activity of the defensive leucocytes of the blood, and the responsiveness of the smooth muscle contained in the small arterioles governing the blood supply to various tissues. But all of these responses to endotoxin represent, not toxic or damaging effects, but perfectly normal responses, things done everyday in the normal course of living. What makes them result in disaster for the animal after the injection of endotoxin is that the host has now turned them all on at once as though in response to an alarm signal. The outcome is widespread tissue destruction, widespread clotting of the blood, and generally death. These responses can be entirely prevented and the animal's health completely preserved simply by lifting out one of the host's own participants in this reaction. If, for example, you deplete the blood of all the circulating leucocytes for a period of time (which you can do with various drugs) or if you temporarily administer heparin in order to prevent blood coagulation, then the endotoxin has no effect at all.

It is not known how endotoxin acts to produce this signal, but the mechanism is evidently a very old one in nature. One of the most sensitive of all the experimental animals that we have is the horseshoe crab. An injection as small as one microgram of endotoxin from any one of our gram negative bacterial pathogens into the body cavity of a horseshoe crab will cause a violent response and death within a few hours. If you look at the horseshoe crab's blood cells (which are called hemocytes) under a microscope during this process, you can see them become enmeshed in dense aggregates of some sort of coagulated protein which is secreted by the hemocytes. Within a few hours the animal's blood flow comes to a standstill and he dies. This seems to represent an enormously exaggerated defense reaction aimed, we presume, at defending horseshoe crabs against invasion by various gram negative bacteria that are their pathogens in the sea. And it may turn out that this is a sensible defense mechanism when used appropriately by the horseshoe crab. Fred Bang at Hopkins has demonstrated that the granules of the blood cells of this creature do contain a coagulable protein which becomes clotted when exposed to very small amounts of endotoxin. One assumes that individual microogranisms invading the tissues of the horseshoe crabs in very small numbers would be easy to trap in a coagulum of extruded protein. But when purified endotoxins are injected into the blood of the animal, this otherwise sensible mechanism becomes a sort of propaganda. It gives the information that bacteria are everywhere, all around the place, needing entrapment, so all of the hemocytes extrude all of their protein and the animal forthwith dies.

Now from the horseshoe crab's point of view, I have no doubt this is a valuable and efficient mechanism for keeping pathogens out. When it works well it doesn't contain any hazard at all. But when barriers are breached and bacteria turn up in the tissues in large numbers, or when purified endotoxin is injected in a laboratory experiment, it becomes a very expensive kind of defense. The defense mechanism itself becomes the disease and the cause of death. By the time that death is about to occur, the bacteria have become, from their point of view, innocent bystanders.

Even when bacteria are frontally toxic and destructive to the cells of the host (as in the case of organisms like the diphtheria bacillus which elaborate what are called exotoxins), there is still some question as to the directness of this encounter. The encounter has some of the aspects of an accident. For instance, the diphtheria bacillus would not in any sense be a pathogen were it not for the capacity of this bacterium to elaborate a toxin which causes, among other things, the formation of a membrane in the throat which results in strangulation in vulnerable patients. We know of no other damaging properties. Even so, the toxin-cell reaction looks like a two-way relationship of great intimacy, involving recognition and precise fitting into the molecular machinery of the cell. Pappenheimer, among others, has suggested that it is as though the toxin were being mistaken for a normal participant in the protein synthesis carried on by the cell. Finally it has to be said that the toxin is not the diphtheria bacillus' own idea but is made by the bacterium under instruction from a virus that infects the bacterium. Only organisms that have been infected and have become lysogenic (the term for this virus or bacteriophage) are capable of producing a toxin. So diphtheria is not simply an infection of a human being by the diphtheria bacillus; it is an infection once removed by a bacteriophage whose real business in life is to infect the bacillus. It is even conceivable, as Pappenheimer has suggested, that the genetic information which enables the virus to induce the bacterium to produce the toxin may have been picked up elsewhere in the course of long intimacy with the human host. This is one possible explanation for the similarity of the toxin to the host cell's own constituents.

*Symbiotic relationships between bacteria and their hosts are much more common than infectious diseases*

It is certainly a strange relationship without any of the straight-forward predator-prey aspects that we used to assume about infectious disease. It's hard for me to see what the diphtheria bacillus has to gain in life from the capacity to produce this kind of a toxin. Diphtheria bacilli live well enough on the surface of human respiratory membranes, and the production of this necrotic pseudo-membrane that occludes the respiratory passages obviously carries the risk of killing off the host and ending the relationship. To me, it doesn't make much sense and looks more like a biological mix-up than an evolutionary advantage.

We were all reassured, when the first moon landing was going to be made, that the greatest precautions would be taken to protect the life of the earth, especially human life, from infection by whatever might be alive on the moon. You will remember the elaborate ceremonies of lunar asepsis that were performed after each of the early landings. The voyagers were masked like surgeons and kept behind plate glass, presumably so that they wouldn't breathe moon dust on the president. They were quarantined away from contact with the earth until it was a certainty that we wouldn't catch something from them. The idea that germs are all around us, trying to get at us, to devour and destroy us, is so firmly rooted in the modern consciousness that it made sense, at that time, to think that strange germs from the moon might be even scarier and harder to handle than our own.

It is true, of course, that germs are all around us. They comprise an astonishing proportion of the sheer bulk of the soil of the earth; they abound in the air and in the water. But it is certainly not true that they are natural enemies. Indeed, it comes as a surprise to realize that such a tiny minority of the bacterial populations of the earth has any interest at all in us. The commonest of encounters between bacteria and the higher forms of life take place after death of the latter, in the course of recycling the elements of life. This recycling, which has nothing at all to do with disease, is, I think, the main business of the microbial world in general.

It is probably true that symbiotic relationships between bacteria and their metazoan hosts, the so-called higher forms of life, are much more common than any infectious diseases in nature. There are the indispensable microbes living in various intestinal tracts, including our own, supplying essential nutrients or providing enzymes for the breakdown of otherwise indigestible food. There are all the peculiar bacterial aggregates that live like necessary organs in the tissues of many insects; if you get rid of these bacteria, the insects die out after a few generations. There are all the bacterial symbionts engaged in nitrogen fixation in collaboration with the legumes of the earth. The total mass of symbiotic microbial life is overwhelming. For sheer numbers nothing can match the enormous population of bacteria or the lineal descendants of bacteria which have taken the form of mitochondria and have become essential symbionts for the production of oxidative energy in the cytoplasm of all nucleated cells, including our own. And there are even greater numbers of the descendants of photosynthetic bacteria which became the chloroplasts of all green plants. Without these two tremendous populations, the mitochondrial descendants of bacteria and the chloroplast descendants of bacteria, neither plant nor animal life

*A tiny minority of the bacterial populations of the earth has any interest in us at all*

as we know it could ever have existed on the earth. In comparison, the number of important bacterial infections of human beings does seem a relative handful.

It might be different for us if we had learned less about sanitation, nutrition and crowding, and particularly plumbing. It is in fact different for the newborn children in places where these things are not handled well. Far and away the greatest cause of infant mortality is enteric infections spread from one human being to another by means of a contaminated environment. But, by and large, infection has become in our kind of civilization a relatively minor threat to life. I suppose it is still a lesser threat now that we have antibiotics.

*In our thinking about cancer, we keep looking for outside causes. We imagine a kind of demonology*

But even before all these developments, in the centuries of the great plagues when times seemed uniformly awful everywhere, the war between microbes and men was never really an event of great biological scale. It was always a funny kind of combat. More often than not the violence of those diseases could also be attributed primarily to the violence of the host's defense mechanisms. Leprosy, like tuberculosis, is a highly destructive disease, but the destructiveness is in large part, perhaps entirely, immunological and under the governance of the infected host. The major lesions of syphilis, including those affecting the arteries and probably those also affecting the central nervous system, are based, at least in part, on the immunological responses of the host to the spirochete rather than to any special habits of the spirochete itself.

Today, with so much of infectious disease presumed to be under control, we are left with a roster of important diseases that it has become fashionable to call "degenerative." These include chronic diseases of the brain and the spinal cord and such things as chronic nephritis, rheumatoid arthritis, arteriosclerosis and various other diseases associated with interference with the circulation of the blood. Although the underlying mechanisms governing these diseases are largely mysterious, I think there is something wrong with the popular view that they are all the results of environmental influences—things we eat, or breathe, or touch. And as is the case in so much of our thinking about cancer these days, we keep looking for outside causes for the things that go wrong. We imagine a kind of demonology.

It will probably turn out, when we've learned more about

mechanisms in general, that most of the events that underlie the tissue damage in these diseases are host mechanisms, under host control. We are vulnerable because of our very intricacy and complexity. We are systems of mechanisms, subject to all the small disturbances and tiny monkey wrenches that can produce the wracking and unhinging of endless chains of coordinated and meticulously timed interactions.

In the end, I believe, we will find that our vulnerability to disease is intrinsic. We are encircled, endangered always, by our own strategies. We live at the mercy of our own armament.

Yet I think we should become more aware that by and large we do live quite well. Considering the kinds of trouble we can get ourselves into and the evidences of internal fragility as we see them in disease, it is nothing short of astonishing that we do so well. It is a surprising and pleasing fact of life that most of us really do go through almost all of our lives, decade after decade, in the best of health. We are not fragile. We do not live as much as we think under constant hazard of internal dissolution. We are in fact well designed, tough, feasible animals. Eventually, of course, we age and wear out, dying in the best of worlds by simply coming to pieces. But we are not struck down. We are not felled from the outside; we fall apart.

The mechanisms of disease are of intense interest, and an entrancing puzzle. But even more interesting and entrancing is the greater mystery of our sustained, enduring, average good health. I wish we had a better feel for how it works. I am less bewildered by why we fail to live for much longer stretches than I am by the miraculous contraption that manages to carry us along for as long as it does.

Why is it that we are not more conscious of our general good health, our almost invulnerability, the near perfection of the fantastic systems of cells and tissues that make us up? Why not a sense of celebration instead of the apprehension of imminent failure under which most of us tend to spend our days? Statistically, the probability that you or I will awake tomorrow with any sort of mortal affliction is extremely low, and yet this small danger is what we are continually reminded of in television commercials, magazine articles and especially in interminable conversations. I think people talk more about illness than any topic except perhaps the weather. How are you? How do you do? How

*We are encircled, endangered always, by our own strategies. We live at the mercy of our own armaments*

are you feeling today? Keeping well? Keep fit. Have a drink to your very good health.

Partly, of course, we are misled by our own propaganda—this century's continuing preoccupation with the fragility of health. But there is something else, another matter hidden beneath the surface, between the lines. It is death, and the act of dying.

I think it is mostly the act itself that we fear so much. To become dead seems to involve so cataclysmic a transformation that it is taken for granted as a dreadful process to go through, agonizing and frightening and filled with horror. It is probably not so. Although we are largely ignorant about the physiology of dying, the sparse information which is available suggests rather strongly that the popular view of dying as agony has it all wrong. Dying may conceivably be exactly the opposite.

Montaigne had a feeling about this, based on his own close call with death in a riding accident. He was knocked unconscious and awoke some hours later while being carried home, thought by his friends to be dead. He writes: "I saw myself all bloody, stained all over with the blood I had thrown up.... It seemed to me that my life was hanging only by the tip of my lips. I closed my eyes in order, it seemed to me, to help push it out, and took pleasure in growing languid and letting myself go. It was an idea that was only floating on the surface of my soul, as delicate and feeble as all the rest, but in truth not only free from distress but mingled with that sweet feeling that people have who have let themselves slide into sleep. I believe that this is the same state in which people find themselves whom we see fainting in the agony of death, and I maintain that we pity them without cause."

Montaigne returns later to this episode; he cannot get it out of his mind. "My condition was, in truth, very pleasant and peaceful. I felt no affliction either for others or for myself; it was a languor... without any pain.... I was letting myself slip away so gently, so gradually and easily, that I hardly ever did anything with less of a feeling of effort. In order to get used to the idea of death," concludes Montaigne, "I find there is nothing like coming close to it." Well, perhaps we have more fear of dying these days, in our civilized world, because of having fewer opportunities to come close to it.

David Livingstone, the British explorer, wrote similarly about his near death. He was caught by a wounded lion, crushed across the right chest and shoulder in the animal's jaws, and very nearly literally worried to death. Rescued at the very last second, he recovered from the injuries and wrote a detailed account of the episode in his memoirs. He remembered the whole thing, from being snatched to being rescued, in vivid detail. There was, Livingstone asserted, no pain or anything at all like anguish or fear. There was, on the contrary, an extraordinary sense of calmness, tranquility and lassitude. He knew precisely where he was and what was happening to him in the lion's jaws, but it did not seem to matter at all. He was so impressed by this experience that he developed the outlines of a theory about being killed, postulating that nature has somehow provided a special mechanism which is turned on at the time of dying, carrying all doomed organisms through in a haze of painlessness and relaxation.

Sir William Osler, who in his time saw a great many people die, was quite firmly convinced about this. He had never seen an agony of death and he maintained there was no such thing. The most recent techniques for resuscitation have led to a scattering of studies that appear to indicate the same thing. People who have dropped "dead" with coronary occlusion and then been revived, or even those who have "died" more slowly from respiratory obstruction, do not speak of agony or fear, or even discomfort. And those who can recall parts or all of the episode remember only a state of calm detachment, with something almost like pleasure in it.

If these impressions are true, could it be that the sensations associated with dying are the manifestations of a proper physiological mechanism? Is there, in fact, such a thing as the "process" of dying? This idea does not seem unreasonable to me, considering the meticulously designed, orderly mechanisms at work in all other important events of living, including those events involved in the initiation of life. It is not unlikely that there is a pivotal moment at some stage in the body's reaction to injury or disease, and maybe in some stage of aging as well, when the organism concedes that it is finished and that the time for dying is at hand. At this moment the events that lead to death may be launched as a coordinated mechanism. Functions are then irreversibly shut off in sequence. Perhaps simultaneously a neural mechanism held ready for this occasion is switched on so that the perception in consciousness becomes like that of Montaigne, or Livingstone, or the resuscitated movie actor who a couple of years ago fell dead with cardiac standstill in front of a Los Angeles hospital and was carried inside to have his heart started again by electric shock. He remembered only his wonderment at the agitation of the people around his stretcher at a time of such tranquility.

If there should be a mechanism for the process of dying, we ought to be on the lookout for pathology in its operation, on the assumption that any intricate mechanism can slip up and be turned on inappropriately. It may be that something like this happens in the well-documented cases of death from witchcraft and hexing. A physician named Milton in Australia has described in **Lancet** lately a fatal syndrome which he calls "self-willed death," occurring in vigorous, previously healthy men when they are informed that they have cancer. Overnight, these patients become apathetic and withdrawn, and within a matter of weeks they die without any satisfactory autopsy explanation for the dying. Milton, as an Australian, was struck by the resemblances between this syndrome and the reported phenomenon of death after "bone-pointing" among Australian aborigines.

There may be an animal model which shows the turning on of the mechanism for dying as the result of pure bad news. Curt Richter, a distinguished biologist at Johns Hopkins, discovered some time ago by accident that rats whose whiskers have been clipped away are peculiarly vulnerable to sudden death when they are placed in water. Instead of swimming on for as long as seventy-two hours as is the case with normal rats, the dewhiskered animals gave up within the first few minutes after being immersed and sank like stones to the bottom, suddenly and unaccountably dead. Richter then found that if these rats were rescued from the water at the last second, just before death, and held for a moment on either a hand or a dry surface, they revived immediately. Surprisingly, they then became capable of swimming on to survival for seventy-two hours, the same length of time as normal rats. It was as if the combination of no whiskers and deep water were a kind of hex, a piece of extraordinarily bad news, a pointing of bones, turning on the mechanism of dying.

And when the hex was cancelled by rescue, the magic vanished and the mechanism was locked up again.

Adam Goldstein has recently reported that there is a substance elaborated in the brain which mimics morphine, at least to the extent that it is selectively bound to the same cellular receptors, chiefly in the brain stem, which are now believed to be specific for the attachment of morphine. Goldstein suggests that a secretion like this, attachable to the same receptors as those which engage the specific groupings of the morphine molecules, might be centrally involved in such things as analgesia, or the failure to sense pain, which is often associated with overwhelming trauma. It is also possible, I should think, that an overabundant elaboration of any substance like this within the brain might itself be involved in the launching of death, either at death's appointed hour, or, as in the case of Curt Richter's rats, inappropriately and earlier on. Either way, this substance would ensure that the act of dying could be, by the nature of things, a painless and conceivably pleasant experience.

This conjecture, I should emphasize, is pure guesswork on my part. There is as yet no hard evidence that this kind of internal secretion by the brain is in fact turned on in the process of dying. But there is pretty good evidence that the stuff is there and ready to be turned on, so it does seem to me a straightforward working possibility.

It seems that we are, by and large, well provided for. We contain our own pharmacopia. We have built-in mechanisms for coping with all sorts of unexpected contingencies, and even with the act of dying. I would foresee a new kind of illumination somewhere in the very distant future, through which our most powerful technology for dealing with human trouble may turn out to be simply a very powerful sort of understanding. As a corollary, I would foresee that when that time comes those in my profession will all be considerably less inclined to meddle, a professional attitude that Montaigne, among others, urged in the strongest terms just a few centuries back.

*Our most powerful technology for dealing with human trouble may turn out to be simply a very powerful sort of understanding*

Lewis Thomas          169

John Todd is a Canadian with a lifelong interest in agriculture and marine biology, an interest he pursued through a formal education in agriculture, parasitology, tropical medicine, comparative psychology and ethology. He has done pioneering work on fish behavior and taught at San Diego State University and Woods Hole Oceanographic Institution. He, Nancy Jack Todd and Bill McLarney founded the New Alchemy Institute in 1969.

world. I rather admire Stewart Brand's statement as he observes the gurus tumbling down the gangways looking for flocks and he asks, "How central is your service?" That's important. That's why, when the statement is made that it all really doesn't matter because the action is elsewhere, shivers just ripple up my spine. I have a mental image of a kind of nuclear brew within which thousands of little children are being stewed. That is this world. I think that we would be derelict in a religious sense to ignore that possibility.

I want to talk about the relationship between mindscape and landscape. We probably all agree that they are interdependent; I should like to suggest that they are very tightly linked. These territories of mind and world shape the future and the future is at stake. The world we live in, our being, and our doing create the territories of our minds. One of the reasons we argue, disagree, and pass right by each other is that these relationships vary so much from person to person. So I think it's important for our understanding of each other to begin with New Alchemy's world view—the way I and others who work with me feel about the world—before we move to the more practical aspects of our lives and our work. I would like to tell a story, a tale perhaps, of New Alchemy as a small-scale, human and holistic science concerned with increasing biological and psychic diversity, and conscious that nothing can or should be separated from anything else. Energy, wastes, the culture of foods, shelter, community, the philosophic sphere—all should somehow be brought together into a form of holism. Though my story is personal, others within New Alchemy have had similar experiences.

I've been in love with the Earth's living mantle since I was a small child. Once I could read, I was enveloped in the theories of a variety of the more visionary agriculturalists like Sir Albert Howard, Louis Bromfield, and J. Russel Smith. While studying agriculture at McGill University, I became quite enthralled with the science of ecology. I moved into parasitology and tropical medicine because I was, by that time, concerned with the ecology of disease, which is an ecology like any other. So after a period of essentially biological training, I became an environmental consultant and had the wonderful task of looking up the rumps of industry for a lot of money for a while before I went on to Ann Arbor in 1964 to work on my doctorate. My field was comparative psychology and ethology, the European science of behaviorism (a type of biological behaviorism), and I minored in oceanography and the study of lakes.

But the really important thing about that experience in Ann Arbor, and I suspect that there were many other people having comparable experiences, was something in the social sphere. This time was the beginning of the anti-war movement and Nancy, my wife, was a very active participant. She, like others in the anti-war movement, was very much into the inness of the world and its very fragile nature. I was working with a variety of scientists who were simply not involved. Their lives, and mine was no exception, were so narrowly organized that they couldn't give up five or ten minutes or an hour to entering into the body politic. At this time I felt conflict about being in a laboratory all day while seeing the world go to hell in a handbasket and doing little or nothing about it.

Yet, since I was able to do some creative research, science wasn't totally negative in my life. I discovered that fish of one particular species were able, without smell, vibrations, sound, and sight, to travel, even to triangulate, through aquatic space by using senses which were like tastebuds all over their bodies. This was taste navigation. When I got more involved in the private lives of fishes, I found that many of them rivaled the mammals in their social behavior. They had complex social organizations, recognition of individuals, and long-term memory; and this behavior was mediated by a chemical language. Animal communication was for me a fascinating field, but all the same I also tried to justify some of my science by working on such issues as the biology of aggression. Nevertheless I was really only playing games on the periphery of significant events.

Well, this conflict led me to question all the values around me—quite common currency at that time. I began by questioning most strongly those closest to home, those of comparative psychology, and realised that implicit in the reductionism and the mechanism of the majority of my work and the work of my colleagues was a very narrow, very arrogant vision of the future. Once I removed myself from that world view, I saw it in retrospect as a very frightening one. After trying to get some understanding of the behavioral sciences, I started to explore the actual relationship between science and society. It became quite clear that there was nothing at all neutral about science; it was really the handmaiden of technology, industry, and society. Furthermore, when I really began to probe more deeply I discovered that, simply by the funding of science, the ideas of a whole generation of scientists can be shaped; projects that seem supportable are encouraged. There is a very tight feedback loop—less tight in some of the natural sciences and extremely tight in some of the physical sciences. There was almost a demonic nature to this course. There were no ethics, no neutrality, not much in the way of morality. I suppose it would be asking too much for these values to exist in science if they didn't in the rest of society, but the scientists' withdrawal from the body politic disturbed me.

By this time, I was a professor teaching ethology to a class of eighteen students in California and thought I was very concerned with what humans were doing to the living component of their planet. I wanted to find out how the subtle behavior and social organization of fishes would be affected by a relatively simple, almost universally used, compound like DDT. I went to the tropical fish stores around southern California and came back with eighteen species of fish. Of these species, some schooled, some aggregated, some took care of their young, some built nests, and some had complex social organizations. There was represented in my sample of species behavior a goodly chunk of the gamut of evolution found in the 27,000 plus species of fishes. I asked each student to introduce minute amounts of DDT into the fish communities, slowly to increase the amounts, and to observe what happened. Well, the findings weren't at all the holocaust I had expected. What happened was that some animals were affected not at all until the DDT reached lethal limits and they just died. I had predicted more insidious changes. Other animals were affected well before they died, as their social behavior was disrupted. Several species of fishes, given just the minute amounts, lost the ability to recognize their young and to transmit and integrate signals; there was, in fact, social chaos. In some species with subtle detection of individuals, there were aggression and murder and mayhem. The more highly evolved the species, the more subtly the fish were tuned to each other and the more vulnerable they were to these minute quantities of stress. Were we really dealing with a perverse kind of reverse evolution?

Well, Bill McLarney and I began a research program in a field we labelled environmental ethology. We explained to the Atomic Energy Commission that they might be doing more damage than they realized, and immediately they supported our research to find out whether this was true. We began to study the effects of social organization, environment, and subtle changes in the biological world. The work was moved from California to Woods Hole, and a special lab was built for us. After a couple of years of work we were able to corroborate the early findings of my students' experiments. Those animals having physiological adaptability but very little behaviorial or social adaptability were able to adapt to and survive under sublethal stress. As species became increasingly complex socially, they also became increasingly vulnerable to perturbations, natural or otherwise (and ours were certainly otherwise), in the environment. We were finally able to develop the idea that a relatively stable ecosystem with a great amount of diversity is an ecosystem where cooperation and symbiotic relationships begin to evolve. It is also the most vulnerable ecosystem.

We had become extremely fascinated by this kind of work, but it was doom-watching and there is nothing constructive and restorative about this kind of research. It did, however, bring us into an international network of other doom-watchers who would meet at various places and describe their findings, saying that this or that pollutant was causing biotic damage. Most of these people were very restricted in their vision, but a few of us felt that we were observing a broader phenomenon. Others agreed completely that the planet was threatened, but felt that science would gallop in and save us. They had the argumentative edge. They had their moon shots and their green revolutions and we had to keep our mouths shut. But what really seemed to be happening was that a crisis was evolving and that crisis was being turned into a commodity—if one process causes a problem, we'll invent another process or add another technology to correct that problem.

We were also dealing with the crisis of crises—the nuclear dilemma touted by many as the solution to our various problems, including the energy problem. I mention this because any planetary consciousness or planetary awareness must take into account the new concern (it's a new concern to me, though some more steeped in mythology might argue it's an ancient concept) that we could obliterate ourselves. I know we've heard this for a long time, but the July 1974 Pugwash Report concludes that nuclear arms are out of control. There are no controls. The so-called test ban treaties are smokescreens. They become very evident as smokescreens when Nixon gives arms away to Israel and Iran, and Canada gives them to India, and every little nuclear reactor that goes to pump up kilowatts on the line (or megawatts on the line as they like to say) is also a plutonium plant. In addition, the kind of knowledge it takes to make these devices is fairly widely available. We have been told by George Wald that, as a student exercise, one guy at MIT built about nine-tenths of a ballistic missile using just available scrap material. Right now nuclear weapons are a seven-billion-dollar business, and no philosophic, no ideological, no political system can comprehend or deal with a seven-billion-dollar-a-year business in the United States. That kind of money just talks too loudly.

The question, "Then where do we go?" has been raised a number of times. This was the question with which some other concerned people and I were confronted when we formed a little group while we were still in California. A number of us were still teaching, and Bill McLarney was writing a book which is now the only comprehensive book in the English language on aquaculture. We went off into the mountains with some of our friends to see if we could create a commune where we could come into harmony with the Earth. The country we chose had big boulders and chaparral; there wasn't much of anything but it was pretty. We wanted to make it partially self-sufficient; in fact, we just wanted to make it work. We discovered, to our horror, that even with our collective boatload of degrees, we weren't able to make that little piece of land work. We didn't know what was going on.

*We discovered, to our horror, that even with our collective boatload of degrees we weren't able to make that little piece of land work*

I said, "Ah, youth, that's what's needed." So I got twelve graduate students and we went roaring out there. The name of the course was how to make this ranch into a biotechnic, autonomous village in harmony with nature. The college catalogue listed the title of the course as "Cold-blooded Vertebrates," but everybody knew what I was about. So we went out there and I said, "We'll spend two weekends walking this place, getting the feel of it, and then we'll really know what to do." Half of them said, "Oh, whee!" and dropped a pack of acid, and the other half, you know—the whole thing. A couple of weeks later we met and there was only one concrete idea given on how to make the land work to sustain a community. A Chinese student who had seen a Japanese bath in one of Stewart Brand's early supplements to the **Whole Earth Catalogue** said, ''Well, at least we can build one of those and all can sit in it.''

This was kind of a crisis point in my life—not the bath, I can deal with that. So I said, ''O.K., something is very much wrong with ourselves and our education, and the only thing I can see to do is to get to know everything out there. There are fifteen or sixteen of us; one's going to find the toads, the others are going to study the trees, the shrubs, birds, mammals, geology, climate, everything.'' We just spread the group out and each person had to study in detail some aspect of the place. They had to work that whole semester and they had to work hard because this was getting serious. It was a calamity; they knew it and I knew it. The other stipulation was that not only were we to create a living museum, but each one had to teach everybody in the class what he had learned. In other words, if someone had figured out all the plants, it was his obligation to teach all of us about the plants.

This went on for several months. Initially there was grumbling. Slowly the dynamics began to change; we were teaching each other. Finally somebody would come and say, ''Do you know, I found a plant down in that little valley over there and I looked it up, and according to the literature it's got to have its roots in water.'' (If you know that country, there ain't any water around there.) Fantastic. Another person found a kind of soil association which semed to be self-renewing and suitable for food farther down the watershed from a live oak area; the first clue was a proliferation of miner's lettuce. We found it was innately fertile soil. A whole variety of tiny, minuscule things like this began to happen to us. Then suddenly, we figured out stable wind currents and found a water source in a cleavage in the side of the hill, its presence revealed by a few plants; we could pump the water up into a series of tiny dams. Fish could be brought into pools behind these dams, and when the dams were opened the silt that formed (there is no soil there) could then be washed out onto the projected gardens below. One after another we began to become sensitive to this particular place and it changed us; I don't think any of us has ever been the same since.

*One after another we began to become sensitive to this particular place and it changed us; I don't think any of us has ever been the same since*

John Todd          177

We learned that you can find the most intriguing allies anywhere you want to look, but it really requires a kind of looking which we're not taught. Ironically enough, it involves a lot of science. We refused to separate anything from anything else; we were beginning to get a glimmering of the power of the microcosm and of the restorative and liberatory nature of holism. So we began to understand, albeit dimly, what was meant by the karma yogi and by many of the alchemists of earlier ages who, by going into the world and working with it, were able to bring about their own personal growth. This first insight into a way of dealing with the world was very satisfying.

So New Alchemy's story began with the realization that none of us and no one we knew had the knowledge or even the wisdom to make a tiny piece of the world work. We came to realize that a number of things about our approach needed changing, and through a series of biological, political, social, and philosophic insights we consciously began to change some of our frames of reference. Almost simultaneously several of our assumptions, both conscious and unconscious, began to change. I believe that it is as possible to change assumptions as to replace hunchbacked scribes with carbon paper.

*Without losing the planetary perspective, we wanted to explore the idea that the microcosm is a knowable mirror image of the larger sphere*

One of our basic shifts has been the reduction of the scale of our being to the point that we can grasp tangible wholes. This concept of scale is terribly important. Somehow a man doesn't feel a bomb landing 3,000 or 5,000 miles away. Somehow an executive who displaces a mountainside farmer in Costa Rica so he can strip mine for bauxite has no immediate feedback. On the other hand, if he throws a rotten apple at his neighbor, he has some idea of the consequences of his act. Without losing the planetary perspective, we wanted to explore the idea that the microcosm is a knowable mirror image of the larger sphere. Alchemy has traditionally dealt with this relationship between the microcosm and the macrocosm; we had the Taoist and Hermetic traditions to guide us. We realized that a reduction in the scale of our thinking would also involve a small-scale attempt to fuse science and practicality with scholarly, religious and artistic pursuits.

Secondly, we wanted to change, as quickly as possible, from hardware-intensive to informationally-extensive strategies. We felt that a move from hardware, in the strict sense of the word, to information would be biologically and politically adaptive. Building a machine requires capital and capital creates haves and have nots. The rich get richer and the poor get poorer. Though it's an oversimplification, the very idea of machinery, of engines, suggests wealth that usually leads to social disparities. Taking something powered by a machine and deriving its power from what is given to us by nature is informationally expensive, but the action, like the recipe in a good cookbook, can theoretically belong to everybody.

Another shift, perhaps very obvious to us but not to a lot of global thinkers, has been the shift from control to participation. Participation is necessary, not only politically, but also for the existence of a perspective throughout the population as a whole. Numbers are important in change. We must insist upon some sort of widespread perspective. Most population biologists would giggle and laugh at our naive assumptions about elites; I don't think they'd be impressed with us. As an example of the difference between control and participation, picture a human being in an elevator on top of the World Trade Center in New York during a brownout. He is psychically about as far removed as possible from the processes which sustain him. Picture the similar person living in such a way that the processes that sustain him or her are in fact being orchestrated by him or her. I think you would see the beginning of more rational decision making and more kindness towards other creatures. An attitude is the end point of a process and I think the shift from one process to another can be brought about consciously.

*We felt that a move from hardware to information would be biologically and politically adaptive*

Another aspect of our thinking has been a change from the monocrop of the world and the mind to a more bioregional approach to the future. If our present global planners have their way, in another decade or two we'll all be living off a tiny bank of genes for rice and wheat. If a pathogen should sweep around the world, we would have virtually no genetic basis for survival. That is monocropping of the world; I think monocropping of the mind is the other side of that planetary vision.

Then our fifth conscious change was the decision to shift from non-renewable to renewable materials. Though that can be considered strictly an ecological act, it's politically loaded.

Sixth, we decided to move from the potentially destructive to the possibly harmless—away from the atom to the wind. I think

John Todd     179

this is a political decision which is necessary if we are to fulfill our obligaton to Gaia or the Earth as an entity with its own problems, not the least of which is humanity.

I'd like to tell you about a few of our crucibles; they are but embryos of what they may someday be. Though each crucible is being studied for a slightly different reason, all are relevant to, or provide metaphors for, the concept of conscious adaptation. We wanted to work initially in two basic spheres—the concept of food and famine and the idea of energy. We were working at the Oceanographic Institute and we set up a small center on Cape Cod and then another small center in California and one in Central America. Though the environment and the people determine the work of each center, there are, surprisingly enough, more similarities than differences. The two tasks we set ourselves were to attempt to reintegrate existing knowledge into an ecological and human framework and to seek forms of knowledge that could strengthen community. These tasks haven't proven in actuality to be quite as distinct as we had originally thought they would. Working with the practical and carrying out scientific experimentation on a small scale has made our relationships with each other and our sensitivity to each other more profound.

*The myth of return to rural life is baloney; we've destroyed our soils. The industrialization of agriculture will not permit us, without a lot of agony, the luxury of going back to 1850*

The first questions we asked ourselves when we got started at New Alchemy were simple ones. It didn't really take much foresight a few years ago to realize that there would be a lot of hunger in the world. When you support only one type of food production by basing agriculture from its fertilizers through to its biocides on petroleum products and you realize what the rates of pumping are, then I think it's very easy to project where things are going to go. In a few years when energy becomes as expensive here as it already is in other parts of the world, millions will be trapped in urban areas with no agriculture to support them. The myth of return to rural life has been mentioned. It's baloney; we've destroyed our soils. The industrialization of agriculture will not permit us, without a lot of agony, the luxury of going back to 1850.

We had to find ways that a small group of people could grow their own food in a tiny place—a rooftop, an alley, or a vacant lot. So we asked ourselves two questions to start with. One, is it possible in a fifty-by-fifty foot space (don't ask us where we got that figure) to produce enough food for the needs of a tiny group of people using almost exclusively nature's strategies, and to do so at no cost once the shell or skeleton is set up? We were ambiguous about the size of the group and ambiguous about the needs but not about the question. It's a biological question, a futuristic question, and also a political question. We next asked another part of the same question — is nature miniaturizable? This gets a bit into the alchemy of the matter. Is it possible to go out into nature and bring back what is necessary to sustain us?

We soon began to realize that one of our major constraints as northern dwellers or as dwellers in arid lands is seasonal pulses. There's not a lot you can do with winter or periods of drought. Winter and drought have produced the storage psychology which caused a lot of the problems that began, some people say, ten thousand years ago. So we thought it would be very nice if we could design a system that would sidestep nature enough to function year around in northern climates. Such a system couldn't bleed freely in and out of the existing world; it would have to be a terrestrial capsule or a tiny place or a bioshelter. Since biological processes are, to a certain extent, temperature dependant, if we had only this tiny fifty-by-fifty foot space we would certainly need to have elevated temperatures. So that gave us the concept of a tropical miniature world, an idea we liked because we could rove the world and come back with little organisms to put inside our terrestrial capsule. If these organisms went outside they would get their butts froze and wouldn't be able to contaminate the native ecosystem toward which we have a very powerful obligation.

*Is it possible, in a fifty-by-fifty space, to produce enough food for the needs of a tiny group of people using nature's strategies?*

Since we had to move away from playing with non-renewable energy, we had to make the sun our ally. So we took the geodesic dome (somebody had to find a use for those New Age structures) and placed it over a pond, and it acts as a very effective solar trap. The angles are such that the sun's light is transformed to heat from the early hours of the day to the late night hours. Domes aren't for storage; heat is quickly lost to the atmosphere. So we decided to base our heat storage on an aquatic system. The plants inside act as absorber surfaces; the pond is filled with phytoplankton (little green microscopic organisms), which also act as solar absorbers; and the water itself stores the heat. So we've created a tropical pond inside the structure as the basis of a food chain.

When you have a pond, you've got to do aquaculture to use the space. We wanted to find an animal, being complete nutritionally, that could be grown in a small space within an ecosystem which would sustain it. So we asked another question: Here we have this green soup, our solar absorptive surface in our hot pond. Now is there an organism that just loves green soup? You can freewheel when you ask simple questions. So we asked Pan what he'd given us North Americans. He came back with a pretty lousy answer—nothing. When the good god Pan came to giving us fish, he'd forgotten to give us an herbivore or an edible vegetarian. But he did give them to South America, Africa, and Southeast Asia. We rejected the Chinese fishes for the time being because the knowledge and technology required to breed them wouldn't be available to people without sophisticated training. The fishes were also slightly harder to care for. But the Rift Lakes of Africa, which cradled humankind, also cradled tilapia—a fish which has been associated with humanity for a long time. There are pictures of them on the tombs of the pharaohs. **Tilapia Aurea,** the species we use, predominated in the Sea of Galilee two thousand years ago. It is even suspected by a number of people to have been the exact species with which Christ fed the multitudes. Tilapia can be bred by anybody. We produce far more algae than the fish can consume so the pond looks like a dense green soup. The fish swim around with their mouths open, and if the temperature is right they reach edible size within three months. They're delicious and have been described by one food writer as the finest-tasting farm-raised fish he'd ever had. So we have an algae-based food chain in an environment with a year-round growing climate created by trapping the sun's heat. It wasn't simple to create but is simple to emulate.

One reason people have had difficulty growing fish on indigenous food cycles in small spaces is that the fish have a natural mechanism for regulating their populations; they give off growth-inhibiting substances whenever the density reaches a certain point. We have been intent on creating densities many times larger than those found in nature. So the pond water is pumped into a bacterial bath and then transformed. Two classes of bacteria, in the presence of oxygen, turn the ammonia and other toxic compounds produced by the fish into nitrites and nitrates which actually feed the algae. So the water, after passing through a little aquatic filter and forest, comes back into the pond purified. Now that the fish "think" they're living in a large lake, they grow quickly. The system in which I do most of my work requires only a few minutes of care each day. Except for the electricity (which we've now eliminated in one prototype) this system costs nothing beyond maintenance and takes care of itself. Miniaturized ecosystems like these demonstrate a new way of viewing food production.

What I haven't described is the fact that these little bioshelters not only grow fishes, they permit year-round growing of terrestrial foods such as vegetables without fossil fuel heating. In a design sense they are the world in miniature.

Is it possible to create bioshelters which can sustain us and can provide us with our energy, our climate, our foods, and our income? This question has many political and bio-social implications. Think of the modern house. It drains you emotionally, physically, and financially because it really doesn't do any of the jobs that houses should do. What if you lived in one that was in fact a miniature world with all the living processes as well as the ability to create energy and provide foods (perhaps even provide enough foods that you would only need to leave to do what you found was valuable)? Some of our critics have called this an elitist kind of research; we don't see it that way at all. We see it as an idea that could ripple out as quickly as carbon paper. We hope, in thinking of the concept of bioshelter, to open up the kind of freedom which could lead to stewardship. Perhaps we could begin to feel less need to exploit the rest of the world and more desire to tend it in a sacred way.

Ultimately, we come home to the question, "Can we make a difference in the world?" And with a hint of the Taoist giggle, I'd say, "Oh, yes, oh, yes..."

Stewart Brand is best known as the conceiver and editor of the Whole Earth Catalogs. He has been associated with the Merry Pranksters, POINT Foundation, the New Games Tournaments, Liferaft Earth and other cultural explorations. He is now the editor of The CoEvolution Quarterly and a sometime consultant to California Governor Jerry Brown.

# The First Whole Earth Photograph

# 15

## Stewart Brand

I took half a tab of LSD on an afternoon in March, 1966, to see what else was worth doing besides the psychedelic thing that was going on at the time and had one of the simpler excursions of that sort I've ever had. I sat around on a roof in San Francisco, vibrating, and got to looking at the skyline, which is sort of lumpy—there are a lot of highrises, as in all American cities. I'd been spending time with Buckminster Fuller, and I don't know what else converged at that point, but for some reason I noticed that the buildings diverged slightly, one from another. It's your standard fisheye perspective when you're stoned, I suppose, but the way I saw it was that I'd been used to thinking of all those buildings as being parallel, and the fact that they diverged signified they were on a surface which was round and, being a circle, went clear around and closed upon itself. In fact, if I turned on my blanket there on the gravel rooftop and looked clear around, it was indeed a circle, a mandala—a nice finite, entire, low-altitude view of the Earth.

And I got locked in (as you'll do with this substance) to a project in which I just sat all afternoon and tried to think of how we could possibly get a photograph of the whole Earth—that is, of the planet from space. I was a big fan of NASA and of the ten years of space exploration that had gone up to that point, and there we were in 1966, having seen a lot of the moon and a lot of hunks of the Earth, but never the complete mandala.

There was nothing else going on in my life then; I was just sitting around in North Beach watching the years go by, so as soon as I came down, I went to work. For about one hundred dollars, I had the phrase, "Why haven't we seen a photograph of the whole Earth yet?" put on a number of buttons. I had a little poster made, which was a star field with a hole cut in the middle, and it also said, "Why haven't we seen a photograph of the whole Earth yet?" Then I went to the library and got a list (from the **Congressional Directory,** I think) of everybody in Washington who counts and their secretaries. There was also a U.N. list and another book which had the various officers in the Soviet Union who were associated with science and space and so on. I got all their addresses—all told there were about two hundred. I sent buttons in the mail to all those people—to Congressmen and their secretaries, to NASA officials, to U.N. officials, to Russian officials, and to Buckminster Fuller and Marshall McLuhan. (Fuller answered and said that it was ridiculous, you can't see more than half the Earth at a time anyway.)

Not content with waiting for replies in the mail, I got a sandwich board, or rather made a sandwich board. (You can't get them—you can't go to a sandwich board store.) It was a plywood thing with buckskin over the shoulders and painted Day-Glo blue with Day-Glo red letters that said, "Why haven't we seen a photograph of the whole Earth yet?" I also got a little tray on which my buttons were arrayed, a top hat with a crystal heart and a flower, and a white jumpsuit. As soon as I had the outfit together, I made my debut over at Berkeley at Sather Gate. [Audience comment: "And nobody noticed."] This was still '66, it was early in the psychedelic thing—people noticed. Mostly they just veered right off. Later they would have come and thought I was selling hot dogs or fruit smoothies or something. At that time a funny thing happened. I sold a lot of buttons at twenty-five cents apiece and probably broke even on the costs. But I also found myself in the middle of a constant, on-going sidewalk seminar, so I got to find out what was going on in science at the time. Berkeley was fairly active, and one of the guys who bought a button was George Field, an astrophysicist I believe. He said, "This is great. I'm going to NASA next week. Can I have five buttons please?" He asked me to come to his class, in which he had just discovered remnants of the big bang, or something like that. And I realized that I was probably six months ahead of the literature just from standing around.

Then I did it at Stanford and ran into some guys from NASA's Ames Research Center, and they had gossip. It was an amazing learning technique for me—you know, you just feed information around, back around, back around. I'd hear a story from one guy and tell it to the next ten; I was just passing it through and selling these buttons.

Then while I was working with artists in New York, I went to Columbia, which was terrific. I had about twenty people constantly shimmering through; very few bought buttons, but there was a lot of talk. One guy came up and whispered in my ear, "I understand you're under orders, but I'd like to talk to you later." I immediately stopped everything to go hear his story. He had a whole bunch of stuff about how Perry or someone had gone toward the Pole and had gone two thousand miles without getting anywhere, and there were tropical leftovers or something. He said the reason they wouldn't let us see the photograph of the Earth was because it was doughnut shaped and they didn't want us to know.

It was peculiar. I had phrased the question "Why haven't we seen a photograph of the whole Earth yet?" to follow the American enthusiasm for conspiracy, the notion that "they" were protecting us or keeping us from something we ought to have. But also it was "we"—it was really our tax dollars, our project that was doing all this stuff in space, and it was a bit odd that for ten years, with all the photographic apparatus in the world, we hadn't turned the cameras that 180 degrees to look back. We had

*We had designed beautiful cameras but no mirrors. Rather strange*

Stewart Brand      187

designed beautiful cameras but no mirrors. Rather strange.

Well, lots of things happened, but one of the nicest episodes occurred a few years later when I was talking to a Mensa group of kids. I was talking about Indians at the time, but I mentioned the whole Earth thing and one of the fathers said, "You're the guy!" He turned out to be an officer, a captain, in some military or other, and it was his job to handle investigations for NASA on the West Coast. He said he had gotten a request from Washington to investigate some character who was distributing literature about photographs of the whole Earth; they wanted to know if it represented a threat to the U.S. government. And very kindly, without revealing his sources, the captain said that he had conducted the investigation and he knew everything about me and my group (which he found to be me and the four walls). He had written back a letter saying, "You've got to understand, Washington, this is California. People here take very strange enthusiasms, and quite often they do it by themselves. I think it's safe to say that this man represents no serious threat to the U.S. government. Signed, Captain so and so. P.S. By the way, why haven't we seen a photograph of the...?"

189

David Spangler dropped out of a science major at the University of Arizona in 1964 to follow an intuitive call to study the esoteric. Since then he has traveled widely, lecturing and working with groups on human and planetary transformation. He was a co-director of the Findhorn Foundation Community in northern Scotland from 1970 to 1973. He is a founder and director of the Lorian Association and the author of Revelation: The Birth of a New Age.

# The Role of the Esoteric
# 16    in Planetary Culture

## David Spangler

I have been asked to address myself to the idea of religion in an age of "post-civilization," which I will do, but I prefer to approach this topic through an exploration of the idea of the emergence of a planetary culture and the image and role of the esoteric in the process of this emergence. There are several reasons for this change of emphasis. As a human being who confronts the meaning and implications of the sacred in his life (and in the life of our world) and as a member of a civilization that does appear to be transforming into something else, I am naturally interested in and concerned with the dual matters of religion and of post-civilization—what the "something else" may be like. However, I am not a practitioner of any one of the orthodox religious traditions in their popular exoteric forms. Neither am I a professional historian of culture and civilization, as Bill Thompson is, able to discuss the future of civilization out of a perspective of its historical roots.

On the other hand, I am deeply committed to the vision of the emergence of a planetary culture based on holistic, life-affirming and spiritual values and principles, and most of my work is involved in exploring and developing strategies to assist this emergence. Likewise, through my lectures and writings, most notably my book, **REVELATION: Birth of a New Age,** and through my work with the visionary, spiritual community of Findhorn in northern Scotland,* I am identified with the esoteric and the metaphysical, or even, in the minds of some people, with the occult side of life. Actually, I am interested in the creative joining of the ideas at the heart of esoteric philosophy with the service-oriented vision and strategies of building a humane planetary civilization: the blending of the deepest intuitions of our hearts and souls with the noblest and most comprehensive aspirations and plans of our minds and intellects.

Let us begin an exploration of this blending with some definitions. First, what do I mean by "the esoteric?" A dictionary says that the word refers to information or experiences which only a few people know or understand, a side of knowledge and reality hidden away from the majority of men and women. For many, this image carries with it suggestions of mystery and elitism, of initiations, secret societies and bands of powerful adepts guarding the unspeakable wisdoms of creation. If knowledge is power, then this image suggests knowlege at its most powerful, by virtue of its exclusivity and its hint of connection with the mysterious well-springs of the universe. Perhaps it is this connotation that surrounds the esoteric with attitudes that either reject or ridicule it or seek to isolate it behind taboos, rendering it all the more mysterious and esoteric in the process. The idea of the existence of a powerful body of knowledge accessible to only a few is frightening. We may be led by this fear to distort the true

*REVELATION: Birth of a New Age, first published at Findhorn in 1971, is currently available in an up-dated North American edition from its publishers, Rainbow Bridge, 3548 22nd St., San Francisco, Cal. 94114. For information about Findhorn, The Findhorn Garden is published as a Lindisfarne Book by Harper & Row, New York, N.Y.

esoteric experience, either by seeking after it for the wrong reasons (i.e., the quest for power or to be one of the elite who are "in the know") or by rejecting it because we do not know how to gain access to it or do not wish to pay the price involved. We may refuse to face the sense of our impotence in this matter; far better, we may feel, to ignore the esoteric side of life than to confront clearly our apparent weakness before it and run the risk of exposing as a possible illusion our image of powerfulness within the world.

This idea of the esoteric as a realm and source of secret and powerful knowledge is, however, largely an illusion itself. The apparent exclusivity of esoteric knowledge—its very "esotericism"—is not due to any intrinsic secretiveness. The universe is an open book to anyone who will take the time and effort and become open and selfless enough to read it. In many ways, creation reveals its inmost secrets to us through its forms and rhythms, its relationships and patterns, if we had the wit and clarity of vision to see them; indeed, as the ancient Hermetic tradition of gnostic and esoteric philosophy affirms in its most famous dictum, "As Above, So Below," these secrets are embodied in our very beings: we are the reality of esoteric knowledge made flesh. We use that knowledge unconsciously (and occasionally consciously) every day in the processes and actions that enable us to breathe, to perceive, to feel, to think, to create, to be and to become.

*The Universe is an open book to anyone who will take the time and effort and become open and selfless enough to read it*

The esoteric is not just a body of knowledge, a compendium of information; it is the experience of our livingness which, when perceived and known deeply enough, allows us to see where and how our individual selves merge, blend with and participate in the Self of our species, of our world and of our whole universe. It is knowing ourselves, who we are and how we function, with an expanding vision of wholeness, understanding that this knowledge, this wholeness, this identity and pattern of actions cannot be bound and contained by any finite form, but must finally pass through the Omega point of universal convergence and include all that is, was, or can be within its scope. It is a knowing gained in large measure through a clear understanding and acceptance of love and faith, and of wisdom in their expression. If this knowing is esoteric, it is only because relatively so few people expend the time, the energy, the effort, the openness and the love to gain it, just as only a few are willing to invest what is required to become a nuclear physicist or a neurosurgeon.

For many people, modern sciences such as physics or molecular biology are esoteric, but we experience the challenge of their effects in such areas as the construction of nuclear power plants or the production of made-to-order test-tube babies through genetic engineering. Likewise, only a few people understand the intricacies of international finance, but we all experience its effects. Though these fields of study and action are "esoteric," we affirm that they represent a reality. Yet, we ourselves and all that we perceive and experience in creation are effects of a deeper reality. It is that reality which esoteric philosophy and practices seek to understand and represent. If we reject or fail to understand the esoteric, is it because this deeper reality is too vague or unreal, or even unimportant, compared to the kinds of reality dealt with by science, technology, economics and politics? Or is it because these latter areas of study and application are less threatening because we can deal with them without the necessity to change? We can deal with them as bodies of knowledge objective and separate from ourselves, as tools of the mind. Such kinds of knowledge and reality can be known by men and women as men and women, whereas the knowledge of the esoteric can be truly known only when we open ourselves to be more than our familiar images of ourselves and our customary patterns of behavior. In short, the esoteric is not a body of knowledge to be learned by the mind but an involvement of ourselves in a deepening of our livingness resulting in transformation. May it not be a fear of such transformation that blocks us from a clear and honest appraisal of what the esoteric represents? If we limit our awareness and acceptance of what lies creatively behind the forms of our material reality and thereby render that awareness esoteric, is it not because we are unprepared to deal with a knowledge which we cannot transform into a tool but which transforms us instead?

*...a knowledge which we cannot transform into a tool but which transforms us instead*

I am asking these questions out of my personal sense that a clear understanding and acceptance of what are now considered esoteric teachings are important for evolving strategies and tactics to deal with current world crises and with the potential emergence of a planetary culture. In so doing, I am aware of the glamor of mystery and power or the image of fantasy and unreality that surrounds these teachings in the public mind. To large segments of the professional community, whether in science, business, education or even amongst the clergy, esotericism is not respectable. In personal conversations with members of these various professions, I have been told of transcendental and mystical experiences, while some professionals have even privately disclosed that they have a background and a current involvement in esoteric studies, in meditation and in exploration of the deeper side of reality. Yet the climate of disbelief and ridicule existing in the professional world, the world that exerts a significant influence on the course of planetary events, prevents these people from speaking out. As a consequence, the insights and values, not to mention the practical techniques, which esotericism could offer in response to our planetary problems are diluted if not actually lost.

This situation is complicated by the fact that esotericism is not a religion nor a unified body of knowledge. Every major religion has its esoteric component, and as Frithjof Schuon points out it is in the realm of the esoteric that all religions find their transcendent unity.* The esoteric deals with the formless side of reality, the oneness or unity which underlies the diversity of manifestation and form. It deals with the subtle relationship between form and essence and with the way in which consciousness may incarnate and express within the former but still rise to find and blend with its limitlessness within the latter. Because there are a multitude of forms in creation, there are a multitude of ways in which the esoteric component of life is expressed.

This leads us to the recognition that there is a sacred and a profane aspect to esotericism. The former is an experience centered in the realization of the oneness and wholeness of creation and of the universality and immanence of divinity. The latter is the collection of forms, teachings, techniques and philosophies that all attempt to lead a person to that experience of unity.

In this category of ''profane'' or ''mundane'' esoterics lie all the popular metaphysical, occult, magical movements that proliferate within the counterculture, as well as the esoteric traditions

---

*The Transcendent Unity of Religions, Frithjof Schuon, 1975, a Harper Torchbook published by Harper & Row, New York, N.Y.

of Eastern and Western religion and mysticism. At their best, these approaches illumine the formless, creative side of nature and help us to relate to it in a way that reveals our own divinity and our role as responsible participants in a universal community of wholeness. At the worst, popular esoteric movements are rife with delusion and deliberate mystification born of the glamor of "secret knowledge," and may be little more than power trips for a few egos at the expense of others, offering the possibility of escape from responsibility and little chance of meaningful transformation. In such cases, esoterics is treated as a body of knowledge and a form of psychological technology rather than as a true spiritual path and discipline demanding clear self-knowledge and transformation. It becomes simply another form rather than the mirror of and the gateway to the formless and the essential. The resulting distortions more than justify the negative image of esoterics that prevails in large segments of our culture.

I will return to this matter, but now I wish to turn our attention to the idea of a planetary culture. After all, this is not a talk on esotericism per se but on its relationship to the emergence of such a culture.* Now we must consider what we mean by a planetary culture.

I suppose it is most simply defined as a culture or a collective consciousness within humanity that transcends currently existing national, cultural and racial boundaries, emphasizing the image of humanity as one united species. It is a culture in which all humanity participates. It is not necessarily or even desirably a culture that obliterates our current cultural diversities; rather, it is a condition in which a plurality of civilizational modes can co-exist

---

*There are many entrances into the esoteric tradition, as well as countless groups and organizations representing their own brand of "ancient wisdom." One excellent route is through the mystical traditions of one's own religion, though the esoteric component is often more evident in the Eastern traditions. Another organization which is doing pioneering work blending esoteric teachings with planetary service is the Lucis Trust; information is available without charge by writing to 866 United Nations Plaza, Suite 566-7, New York, N.Y. 10017. The work of the Austrian mystic and scientist Rudolph Steiner is another good entry point; one may also wish to examine some of the publications of the Theosophical Society. Finally, the work of the Lindisfarne Association and of William Irwin Thompson directly deals with planetary culture and the esoteric traditions. Whatever route is selected, an open mind blended with discernment and common sense is an essential traveling companion.

and co-relate in synergy rather than in competition, creating a wholeness that is greater than the sum of its parts. It is a culture based primarily on our common humanity and our joint sharing of the biosphere of planet Earth and secondarily upon our particular geographical and cultural identities, like a family in which each person is different and unique but linked by a shared heredity. On a practical economic and political level, it would mean a culture that can use the resources of the earth for the benefit of all humans everywhere—and by this I mean the resources of human consciousness and inventiveness as well—without creating unequal patterns of distribution and sharing due to the self-interest of nation-states or the competition between one region and another.

Although there are many different variations of this image and different suggested routes towards its attainment, this definition of a planetary culture is fairly straightforward and understandable. It is well within the limits of reality as we are accustomed to it. I now want to suggest a second, complementary definition of a planetary culture, but this one asks you to extend your conception of reality, to think esoterically for a moment. This defines a planetary culture as one capable of embodying—giving form and incarnation to—the soul and identity of our planet, just as your body gives form and incarnation to you, to your soul and identity.

*Planetary culture is based on our common humanity and our sharing of the biosphere of the planet Earth*

One of the ideas found in almost all of the esoteric traditions is that our planet is a living being, possessing a consciousness and a soul or a quality of divinity. We speak of Mother Nature or of Gaia, the Earth Goddess. One of my earliest mystical experiences, one, in fact, which directed my life into exploring and communicating the esoteric side of reality, was of contacting and blending with this Being and, in perceiving the infinite love it held for humanity and for all forms of life and matter within its embrace, of seeing us both as its children and as participants in its ongoing creative endeavors. Out of this and subsequent experiences came an image of humanity as a process through which earth was embodying a deeper consciousness of itself; we were like the brain of the planet. At the moment—especially in the Western cultures, but in all cultures to some degree—we are acting as if we live **on** the planet and can use it as a form of quarry; we have no culture that is truly attuned to and part of the planetary Soul or Identity. Now, however, in the turmoil of the convergence of cultures and in the impact of mounting planetary crises, particularly in the ecological domain, we have a chance to see more wholly, to form more holistic images not only of ourselves as humans but of ourselves as part of a seamless planetary garment, a web of interrelationship extending throughout all forms of life and matter and linking us as one. We can begin to see our world in more profound—more esoteric—ways. We can build a culture, or cultures, that exist for the benefit and wholeness of all lives, not just the human, and which can say with understanding that they are instruments through which the will and consciousness and intelligence of the Being that is Earth and of all the beings, including ourselves, which its life embraces and nourishes can be knowingly advanced towards fulfilment.

The achievement of such a planetary culture or planet-attuned, planet-embodying culture is more than a political, economic or cultural effort; it is more than a religious effort, if we think of religion primarily in an institutional sense. It is a spiritual effort. It is a change in the way we see ourselves and our world. It is a transformation of our consciousnesses and of our way of being in and with our world.

It is an effort to see into reality more clearly and more deeply so that what is now considered esoteric will become exoteric in our awareness and our behavior.

It is my conviction that the threshold on which we as humanity now stand is more than one of learning how to cross over to a planet-wide civilization, a new state of human political, economic and cultural unity, however desirable that may be. Such a step is important, but it is only one foot over the threshold if we are viewing our cultures, our civilizations, as expressions of our own humanity exclusively and do not recognize how earth herself is the true culture, the true civilization created and shared by all forms of life. Can we learn to see our planet as the culture or as the seed of that culture? Can we see how all the elements of civilization which we consider culture are reflections of what earth and all its lives have always been creating? Can we see our cultures as more than a human product and as a way of participating in and contributing to the true planetary culture? We are a subculture. In fact, at the present time, one might almost say that we as humanity, especially in our Western mode of being, are a counter culture, so completely have we tended to disregard and devalue the well-being and the biological, ecological, geological civilization of our planet. Now, I feel, we must learn how to unite not only as human beings but also as participants in planetary civilization; we must learn how to transform our species subculture into a true representation and embodiment of the holistic life and culture of our living world. In so doing, I am convinced we will touch qualities in our own beings and will discover greater dimensions to our own identity as humanity which will open areas of growth and achievement of which we cannot now conceive.

It is interesting at this point to consider the original subject of this talk: religion in an age of post-civilization. Civilization arose with the development of agriculture which allowed men and women to settle in relatively permanent locations and to cease being nomadic. With the development of such settlements, which grew into towns and cities, new classes of occupations could arise which were not directly related to the growing and tending of crops but which met the needs of the settlements themselves. In small but emerging ways, human beings began to relate to a world significantly, if not exclusively, of their own creation, as distinct from relating to the world of nature. In de Chardin's terms, the noosphere began to develop. Civilization became in large part, then, the development of a human world distinct from the natural world. Since cities were the focal points and culture beds for this human world, civilization also became the history of the city and of the conflict or competition between the city and the country, the urban dweller and the rural farmer.

*Civilization became in large part the development of a human world distinct from the natural world*

The industrial revolution and its technological offspring have vastly accelerated this process, even to the point of turning agriculture into an industry semi-independent of nature's ancient rhythms. In Western societies, the farmer has become a vanishing species, replaced by the agri-businessman and the agri-technocrat; the city in its broadest sense, as a pattern of consciousness and behavior, has swallowed up the farm and the country; civilization has won and the human world has enveloped the world of nature.

Or so it seemed. But lately we have begun to realize that we have bitten off more than we can chew, that the civilization of the city is only a part of the greater civilization of the planet, and that in any contest between them, earth must win. In reaching its apex, civilization has reached its end, heralded by the warnings of environmental and social degradation and decay. The human world cannot embrace the planetary world; the part cannot swallow the whole. But the part can learn to become the whole, to embody the essence of the greater identity and thus to participate in that identity. This, to me, is the meaning of post-civilization: not necessarily an end to cities as a form, nor an end to the human world, but an end to exclusivity, to fragmentation and to our misidentification of the part with the whole. In revisioning our nature and our identity, we can see that the same creative power that enabled us to build our world, our civilization, is inherent in the earth and is responsible for the creation of all its forms, including ourselves. Perhaps we may call it the universal spirit of divinity or of life. Whatever we call it, it is the point of new perception through which we may learn how to blend our world with the world of earth so that the two may add to each other and a new world, a synthesis or a synergy, may emerge.

What role does religion have in this post-civilization? Religion, to me, is the approach we take to the Phenomenon beyond all phenomena, the Source; it is a way of entering into the holy space of Divinity where revision and re-formation is possible. "Behold," says the Christ, "I make all things new! In Me, all things are possible." A living culture, a culture open to transformation and growth, must learn how to enter that space and act from within it.

In all our religions, there is the tradition of the Divine Incarnation or the approach of Divinity to humanity. If I may offer a prediction, it is that in an age of post-civilization, based on a harmony between humanity and earth born of a vision of their common identity, the sense of such an incarnation will be very important. The Indian sage Sri Aurobindo, around whose work the planetary city of Auroville is being created, spoke of the divinization of matter and of the responsibility of humanity as earth's most highly developed intelligent form of life in making that divinization possible by being a living channel between God and earth. Other seers and prophets have echoed this vision. I believe it will become an important vision for our future, asking us to find ways through which we as individuals and as families, as groups and as institutions, as cities and as cultures may embody the spectrum of identity as widely and wholly as possible, extending the limits of our humanity into the beingness of our world and its other life-forms, our planetary brothers, and beyond, until we are linked in consciousness and action with the source of our divinity. We will seek to find ways through which we, individually and collectively, may incarnate the will and love, wisdom and intelligence, purpose and life of universal divinity.

We have few images in our culture that can give us a sense of what that would be like or of how to achieve it. Our religions, especially in the West, have taught us more of God transcendent than of the God within us and of our own power to incarnate divinity. We have mythologized and deified such examples as we have had within our human family of what it may mean to be such an incarnation or, at the least, to practice the Presence of God. Now, I believe, our religious impulses must turn to help us understand what it means to participate in divinity or to embody the spirit of holiness and wholeness in the context of a dynamic, growing, creative human and planetary culture. We must learn how to participate in the Sacrament of Incarnation and to discover the transcendent elements of human beingness which make our incarnations more than just exercises of the flesh.

This leads me back to the image of the esoteric, for it is precisely this area of perception and insight which teaches us to go beyond forms and to contact the essence of life. The esoteric tradition is precisely the tradition of how we as human beings may participate in and embody the divinity that is our Source and our heritage.

Words may deceive us here, so I wish to reiterate that the esoteric is not a body of knowledge (except in what I have called its "profane" aspects) but an aspect of reality which we have not fully looked at as yet. It is instructive to remember that geometry, certain forms of algebra, astronomy, and certain areas of physics and chemistry were once considered esoteric and occult knowledges. The fact that the earth was round and that it circled the sun was known to both Eastern and Western initiates in esotericism long before Columbus, Copernicus and Galileo demonstrated those facts for their cultures as a whole. Yesterday's esotericism is today's common knowledge. Even now, modern physics confirms the teachings of ancient metaphysics that the universe is a oneness and that thought may be the only reality.* The first step for Columbus in sailing beyond what was

*The esoteric is not a body of knowledge but an aspect of reality which we have not fully looked at as yet*

***The Tao of Physics,** Fritjof Capra, Shambhala Publications, Berkeley, Cal.,

David Spangler     201

thought to be the edge of the world was to perceive and to understand that it could be done because the world was in fact round. The first step for us in creating a planetary culture that is an incarnation of our—and our planet's—divinity and deepest potentials is also to perceive and to understand that it can be done because such divinity is real, such potentials are real, and we have the capacity to do it. The essence of the esoteric tradition, the true image of the esoteric, is precisely this vision of reality. Humanity is a oneness. There is a planetary Soul or life. The two can relate consciously in harmony and in release of unimaginable power and potentials based on mutual love, respect and service to a universal wholeness.

In our professions, in our lives, in our cultures we stand on the threshold of a deeper, more profound, and more freeing insight into ourselves and into our world. We hesitate. Why? What prevents us from moving, from proclaiming a new vision and from rising powerfully and joyously to embody it? Certainly there is the force of inertia, the comfort of the known and the familiar, the security of our vested interests. We are afraid of what we may lose. But this, by itself, would not stop us, I believe, if we fully grasped or allowed ourselves to grasp the promise and potential of what lies before us, especially since we are confronted with alternatives of planetary war, social degradation and ecological disruption and stand to lose everything anyway if we continue without change the course of our civilizations. Men and women have pioneered in the past, and I don't believe we have lost the inherent spirit or strength to do so again if a frontier is clearly perceived.

Another potential barrier to new vision is something I have frequently encountered in persons in the course of my work, and that is the fear of the transcendent or the sublime, which is really the fear of change and of the loss of what is known. It is also based on a curious definition of humanity that says that limitation, fragmentation, pain and suffering—in short, the image of the tragic hero, isolated but strong in his proud and painful individuality—somehow constitute the meaning and glory of being human. To become divine or holistic is to lose that and in some

deals with the parallels between modern physics and Eastern mysticism. Also, a Dutton paperback, **Space-Time and Beyond,** by Bob Toben approaches the same subject from a slightly different angle.

fashion to become insipid. Yet, there is nothing insipid about the universe and its infinity. We have been fed on false models that pit divinity against humanity, forgetting that our individuality is our transcendency brought into a focus, and that both divinity and humanity are a wholeness, just as the universe is a wholeness. To accept and to seek to embody more fully our divinity is to seek to become more of our whole selves, which is a direction towards greater power, greater glory, greater fulfilment and greater meaning, as well as towards greater loving and wiser participation in life than anything which is a fragment of ourselves can offer.

Inertia, vested interests, the fear of change and of losing our humanity (when, in fact, we may only just be beginning to find it) may all block or inhibit our movement towards a new consciousness and a new way of being, but I feel that of equal power to inhibit us is the negative or distorted image we may have of the esoteric. For as we are driven by the very evolutionary force of our civilization to confront new perceptions of reality, we discover that in some cases the only models we have for integrating and understanding these perceptions come from the esoteric traditions, both inside and outside the religious traditions. Yet, we don't want to be considered esotericists (which may be a polite way of saying ''kooks,'' ''weirdos,'' or ''nuts''). We are bound by our need for respectability. Or we may feel that esotericism, while all right in its place, has no part in the ''real'' world of finance, politics and social policy. Also, we may be turned off by the many bizarre forms which the impulse towards the esoteric can take.

It may help if we realize that the esoteric is really a form of language, a way developed by persons through the ages to talk about the deeper aspects of human experience. Now, those deeper aspects are beginning to surface, and we desperately need a clear way of talking about them. The language of esotericism, which is highly symbolic and which in part developed out of a need to protect the concepts involved from being taken out of a living context and into a purely informational one, may not be the language we need, but it can contribute to the evolution of a new way of talking about a new way of being. At any rate, a dialogue is needed. The people involved in forming and implementing new images of society need the insights and need to understand the aspect of reality, the nature of reality, presented in the highest of esoteric traditions, while the people involved in exploring and expounding on that aspect of reality need the input of clear and service-oriented thinking. Too many esoteric groups have almost a siege mentality, born of being involved in a non-traditional world view, and there is too little clear and precise thinking. Ancient metaphysical traditions and systems of practice are dredged up, mixed with elements of magic and ritual, blended with personal needs and glamors, and the result is a true obscuration of what esotericism seeks to reflect.

We are a culture in transition, looking for a new way of being in the world that affirms us as persons and manifests harmony with our planet. The esoteric tradition speaks of such a way of being, grounded in a holistic and profound view of the nature of life and of the identity of humanity in relationship with the identities of Earth and of God; it is looking for a culture that can give its vision substance for the blessing and unfoldment of all the planet. We must learn to bring the parts together, discarding what is spurious, limiting and out of date. The place to start is with the realization that just behind the forms of our world and of our fragmented humanity lies a reality of wholeness, and the power to translate that wholeness into action. This reality infuses the true image of the esoteric, and we need to learn to see this beyond all our hesitations or the distortions of this image. In the image of the esoteric lies a key to the vision of a planetary culture and to a strategy of emergence. Let us explore them both with wisdom and with love on behalf of the new world that struggles to be born.

William Irwin Thompson is a writer, teacher and cultural historian who has taught at Cornell, MIT and York University. His books include At the Edge of History, Passages about Earth and Evil and World Order. In 1973 he left the university to found and work full time with the Lindisfarne Association.

# Notes on an Emerging Planet

# 17

## William Irwin Thompson

In this talk I would like to follow a musical structure of **aria da capo** to go back to where we started in this conference with Gregory Bateson. I would like to try to relate Gregory's attempt to create a new epistemology to the challenge of creating a new culture.

You remember that Gregory was saying that epistemology is timebound thinking. He was talking about the difference between the temporal ''then'' or ''therefore,'' and the atemporal ''then.'' He was concerned with certain kinds of logical as opposed to causal relationships. In this point, Gregory was playing with some of the ideas of Hume on causality and customary conjunction. In considering the rapid leap from **this** to **that**, Gregory wanted more time; he wanted a slowing-down of progress for tentative assimilation and adaptation. He wanted to see more space in which to evolve without this instant crystallization into the rigid cultural forms and institutions which obstruct the flow of time and obstruct the process of evolution. Old mutations fossilize into institutions which have somehow survived their death. So Gregory made a wish that there be no irreversible change except over a long period of time. In this sense, Gregory was being Darwinian and hoping for great expanses of time for slow, incremental mutations.

Now I think the space to create cultures without having them brought into existence in immediate activity is the Imagination. Imagination is that kind of space in which you can create a culture and then play around with it, almost as an M.I.T. engineer would design a vehicle on the sketch-pad TV tube and then play around with it by telling the computer to rotate the structure, turn it inside out, put it under stress. The engineer can play with the airplane and fly it before it has ever gone into hard metal. What the computer sketch-pad is really, is an externalization of the human faculty of the Imagination. Some scientists like Nikola Tesla, for example, could do without a computer and never need to use blueprints. He could see every machine he designed in absolute concrete detail. Mystical visionaries can see their thoughts; George Bernard Shaw, in speaking of St. Joan, said that this ability to see one's thoughts, this ability to have visions, is what separates the mystic from the normal man or woman. The mystic, be he scientist or saint or both, sees his thoughts in a vision, and thus the visionary space becomes a place to escape ''timebound thinking.''

The way to escape timebound thinking is to go through the gate to the Imagination. Remember Munisri kept talking about how in Jain meditation one becomes the gatekeeper, watching at the gate as the thoughts go by without being or identifying with the thoughts going by. Well, the interval between each heartbeat is the gate. Between each heartbeat, and what is the heart but the organ which binds us into time with its pulse and calls us back to the world in love? Between each heartbeat is the opening, the gate to Imagination, to the Visionary Worlds. That unbound timeless interval is the gateway to other possibilities.

Now this conference at Lindisfarne has been, in a sense, a cultural space in which to imagine a new world without rushing it into production, without immediately fossilizing it into institutions, without creating a monument against which we have to bang our knees and get in the way of one another. Lindisfarne is a space in which we have played with time. We've had "the month-long week," as Tom Robertson has said. This overload, this intensification of time in the conference is a way of playing around with time; but we've also had the slowness of time in the interval between each heartbeat or each breath in meditation, as well as the fast dancing in the evening till three o'clock in the morning. All of these are ways of playing with time and ways of escaping timebound thinking. For as Pir Vilayat said, "Time is the measure of our limitations." We must not necessarily take limitations as a negative thing, because limitation is the form which describes the possibilities of an existence. Without limitation there is form spread to infinity and you end up with entropy and the heat-death of the universe. Limitation is the very principle by which the many can come into existence out of the One, or "the unlimited" of Anaximander.

So we have found a way in this Way, and this Way rhymes with the Chinese **Wu-Wei**, the doing of non-doing, in thought as well as sound. We have found in this month-long week of the conference that we **are** more than we **know**. Throughout the conference we have observed the relationship between an individual's knowing and his being. Now if we see this relationship between our full being and our knowing, we come back to another of Gregory's points in the essay on "Conscious Purpose." All the contents of consciousness, our knowing, cannot get on the screen of consciousness. If you had a TV monitor telling you everything about the process of itself and its electrical structure, it would have to have a larger screen to tell you about that process, and in order to do that it would have to have a larger screen; and so we end up with a regress **ad infinitum.** Therefore, the screen of consciousness is limited. It is limited by time, for "Time is the measure of our limitations." It is limited by space, and its knowing must, by definition, be always less than its being. And so the tragedy of human existence is the way in which these opposites cross. They can cross in terms of crucifixion; or, at the heart of the cross the rose can bloom, in the terms of esoteric Christianity.

Now, if all the contents of consciousness cannot get on the screen of consciousness, and, as Gregory says, our small minds deal only with a skewed sample of events of the total Mind, then we create out of our knowing, cultures that are less than our Being. We begin to live, not in reality, but in a description of reality. This is a point that Gregory has made, it's a point that Don Juan makes in the books by Castaneda, and it's a point that Heisenberg makes in his essays on the meaning of the Quantum Theory. Heisenberg says we do not have a science of nature, we have a science of our knowledge of nature; we do not live in nature, we live in our description of nature. There are no such things as elementary particles. An elementary particle is what happens when you build an accelerator; when you decide to chop up the universe in that way, particles are what you get. But if you continue the process to its ultimate extension, matter disappears and you end up with pure abstract patterns and qualities like "charm" and "strangeness." So we end up with a universe in which matter dissolves into music, into pure forms, into geometrical patterns, and this, of course, is basic to what Gregory says in "Form, Substance, and Difference."

I want to go back to the Gospel according to Gregory, because I have felt at times during the conference that he wasn't really being understood. I would hate to have him go away with the feeling that we didn't understand him. So let me read a short bit from "Form, Substance, and Difference."

> If I am right, the whole of our thinking about what we are and what other people are has got to be restructured. This is not funny, and I do not know how long we have to do it in. If we continue to operate on the premises that were fashionable in the pre-cybernetic era, and which were especially under-lined and strengthened during the Industrial Revolution, which seem to validate the Darwinian unit of survival, we may have twenty or thirty years before the logical **reductio ad absurdum** of our old positions destroys us. Nobody knows how long we have, under the present system, before some disaster strikes us, more serious than the destruction of any group of nations. The most important task today is, perhaps,

to learn to think in the new way. Let me say that **I** don't know how to think that way. Intellectually, I can stand here and I can give you a reasoned exposition of the matter; but if I am cutting down a tree, I still think "Gregory Bateson" is cutting down the tree. **I** am cutting down the tree. "Myself" is to me still an excessively concrete object, different from the rest of what I have been calling "mind."

Now the extension of Gregory's point is that if our being is more than our knowing, our interpretation of ourselves is only a description of ourselves, and our interpretations are inadequate descriptions of ourselves. As you come out of an inadequate interpretation of yourself, you realize the inadequacy of your interpretation of others. No one is really equal to his own interpretation, and so the first way of discovering the inadequacy of your interpretation of others is to realize that your own interpretation of yourself isn't really commensurate with what you are. The step to realizing, to making habitual the other way of thinking, so that one naturally thinks that way when he cuts down a tree or reaches for a glass of water, that step is not an easy one. And that is why I think it's important to take animism seriously, and why I spoke to Sean Wellesley-Miller last night about the role of the recovery of animism in post-industrial societies. Along with animism, Taoism and the mystical paths come in to play a role in our advanced electronic society. And, quite seriously, I suggest to you that we should trust no policy decisions which emanate from persons who do not yet have this habit. We must not let anyone near the political process who has not stepped out of small mind and encountered the fullness of Being. If he is still operating from the same old limitations of the ego, he is going to generate chaos. The political implications of this are really immediate and pressing. We must go back to a Taoist model of the role of wisdom, not expertise, in culture, the doing of non-doing, the **Wu-Wei** of the statesman.

*We must go back to a Taoist model of the role of wisdom, not expertise, in culture*

We are being told by "the policy sciences" and Management that we can control the planet through new tools, new technology, and new managerial techniques. But the "policy sciences" and the philosophies of Management are simply linear extensions of the old tools and the old ideas. We are in the middle of a revolution of consciousness, a "paradigm-shift" in science. We are not talking about adding new contents to the structure of the old consciousness, whether these contents are computers or Program Budgeting Systems; we are talking about going back and changing the very structure of consciousness, and this can be done very simply without computers, without even pencil and paper. It can be done in the interval between each heartbeat.

Now as Jonas Salk tries to develop the idea that there is a new consciousness arising, he gets into very different political geography from Gregory. Let me read you something from Jonas's work, **The Survival of the Wisest:**

> A new body of conscious individuals exists, expressing its desire for a better life for Man as a species and as individuals, eager to devote themselves to this end. Such groups, when they are able to coalesce through an understanding of their relatedness to one another and to the natural processes involved in "Nature's game" of survival and evolution, will find strength and courage in sensing themselves as a part of the Cosmos and as being involved in a game that is in accord with Nature and not anti-natural. These groups will initiate movements which, in turn, will be manifest in their effects not only upon the species and the planet but upon individual lives. Their benefit is likely to be expressed in a greater frequency, or proportion, of individuals finding increasing satisfaction and fulfillment in life.

Here you have a kind of evolutionary process where maladaptations generate psychosomatic diseases, the bad news which Lewis Thomas was talking about, and people begin to get so demoralized that they just quit and die. But those who have a positive, buoyant and self-actualizing sense of the joy of existence, those who know with Blake that energy is eternal delight, create new spaces and move into them in the joy of evolving. Now you would think that those of us who live here at Lindisfarne would say about Salk's ideas: "That is really great! That's just what we're trying to do here. Lindisfarnians are Epoch B'ers. We're going to split the planet into the old people of Epoch A, who can't really swing with what is happening, and the people who are now into Epoch B." But that is itself a very Cartesian and very polarized mode of thinking. It splits humanity into the Elect and the Damned, and it has political implications which, I think, are dangerous. As Jonas goes on to say:

Under such circumstances, mass disaster would be expected to ensue, out of which might arise a new variety of Man from a hardy core with the strength and capacity of their Being to adapt to the changed circumstances. **Such individuals might prove to have possessed "the wisdom" to survive.**

Now the difficulty with this idea is that it is a theory of elites. It's talking about the emergence of an evolutionary elite on the planet where the elite forges ahead into a new adaptation and becomes the consummation of the evolutionary process and an intensification of the species as a whole. The Elite become the new policy-makers, the new politicians, the new humanity, the new homo sapiens. Now, I think there are real problems in this view and that this philosophy could be used as the ideology of a new globalist elite. This globalist elite could then make a rapprochement with the multinational corporation executives to introduce a new authoritarian world-order.

Another apologist for evolutionary elitism is Teilhard de Chardin. Chardin's thesis is that hyper-collectivization leads to hyper-personalization. If you have the Church, you can become a Michelangelo or a Palestrina; without the Church, you are just a slob on a desert island trying to whistle in sonata form when you've never even heard a sonata. For Chardin, it is collectivization which gives you your humanity. This idea can become the ideological camouflage for multinational enterprise. The peasant who gives up his tortillas for Ritz Crackers and Coca-Cola can be made to say: "With this purchase I belong to the planet, to the collective. My buying is a form of relating to global society. I don't want to make my own tortillas out of local corn or to live within the integrity of my own ecology; I want to belong to the fullness of humanity, and the only way I know how to do that is by buying Coca-Cola and Ritz Crackers."

So we have to be very careful about the political implications of the ideas we're throwing around in our enthusiasm for "the New Age" or "The Survival of the Wisest." Chardin can become the apology for multinational corporations, and Salk can become the apology for the emergence of a new General-Systems, Globalist Elite. Goethe and Laplace made their peace with Napoleon and hoped for a vision of a United Europe. I think a new race of planetary intellectuals would make their peace with a new

William Irwin Thompson     213

planetary Napoleon. I think we need to be wary of the intellectuals, especially the university intellectuals, who have a lot to hold on to in their positions and their salaries. The professors are likely to be the first ones to fall in line as apologists for the new system. George Wald, at the New Alchemy Institute a week or so ago, said, "Intellectuals think they create the policy, but actually they always follow where the policy goes and simply apologize for it." So we have to be very careful with this notion of elitism in the rise of the mutants of Epoch B who forge ahead into a new adaption.

But if we go back to Gregory's ideas on evolution, I think quite different political implications emerge. If we go back to Gregory's discussion of conscious purpose, we can set up a parallel analogy concerning elites. If all the contents of the mind cannot get onto the screen of consciousness, we can also say that all of the contents of the species, of humanity, cannot get onto the screen of conscious policy and cannot be compressed into a managerial elite. An intellectual elite is the conscious mind or ego of the species, so that everything Gregory is saying about conscious purpose can be said about elites, the agents of conscious purpose.

Now I would extend the idea even further to say that the ideology of an elite cannot express the truth; it can only present, as Gregory would say, a skewed sample of events. An ideology is like a magnetic field with only one pole. The Truth, or the Tao, is what overlights the conflict of opposed ideologies: Gregory Bateson and Jonas Salk, Jonas Salk and Rhoda Lerman, Sean Wellesley-Miller and Leonard Duhl, or myself and Lyn Radzick from Findhorn. Now when we see these oppositions occurring, we tend to get a little uncomfortable, but if we really look at them, we'll notice that an energy comes out of them in which the individual grabs on to his own hidden resources and rises to a new level of eloquence. What we see in these oppositions is what Blake meant when he said, "In opposition is true friendship." The Tao overlights these opposites and the Tao is not expressed in one position or the other. The truth is at a higher level than ideology; as Yeats said on his death bed, "Man cannot know the truth, the truth can only be embodied in him." I think this is a very important point because it means that you cannot formulate a program for your World Order Party. You cannot formulate a simple policy as an ideology; you have to allow for the dialectical play of opposites, elites and non-elites. If you're going to think enantiodromically, the first thing you have to do is to reflect things in the mirror when a policy comes forth. For example, if we take Nikola Tesla's idea of vibrating the whole earth to generate wireless power, power without the problem of transmission lines, then we first consider the image, and then the shadow. If you could go on top of a mountain into a cabin, throw a switch and have power, then you would not need concentrations of populations in cities, which means that wildness would not be protected and a thin film of human settlement could cover the earth like an oil slick. If you had to vibrate the whole earth to generate that power, then you would have to consider what that might do to the earth's magnetic field, the Van Allen Belts, the solar wind. If you move up to a planetary scale of good, you are also creating a planetary scale for evil.

The difficulty is that all policy makers think in linear fashion. They think in terms of good guys and bad guys, and feel that if they could come into power, all would be right. However, we have seen all through history that changing the faces of those in power does not change the structure of the contradictions of human culture. So we have to come back to what Gregory was talking about: we don't simply add a new content, and change from capitalist to socialist; we change the way we conceive reality. We go behind the content to understand the structure of consciousness to see how the enantiodromias flip back and forth through space and time.

Now as we look at the conflict of opposites within this conference, this space for the Imagination to come into being, we can see that there have been certain moments of truth. Gregory did not speak **the** Truth; Jonas did not utter **the** Truth; Rhoda did not proclaim **the** Truth; the moment of truth overlighted the energy-field when Gregory disagreed with Jonas, or when Jonas disagreed with Rhoda. Our first response is to dislike resistance. We fail to see that resistance is necessary to the integrity of a force; the resistance of the stone sharpens the blade. If we love our enemies, then we see that the opponent draws us out of the inchoate mass into the fullness of being.

Now when we see these moments of truth, we come upon a pattern, not an object or an ego; thus the basic unit of consciousness is a union, a relationship—the organism plus the environ-

*If you move up to a planetary scale of good, you are also creating a planetary scale for evil*

William Irwin Thompson          215

ment is the basic evolving unit, according to Gregory. And so what both Gregory and I are trying to get at is that the basic nature of reality is not substance, it's pattern, relationship, a field. The universe is made out of music, not matter; matter, like a crystal or a cathedral, is simply "frozen music." Recall Gregory's question concerning the basic unit of information by which the frog knows how to arrange the symmetry of its leg. How is that information translated in the cell? The information seems to be pure pattern. Is the hand a notation for "produce five fingers" or "produce four angles"? Is the fist an object, or is the fist a relationship? What is the difference between a hand and a fist? Obviously, it's a performance, a process in Whitehead's sense. The fist is not an object. So we have to look at reality in a different way and can begin to see why the Eskimos have twenty-five different words for snow. So we come down to patterns, to "Form, Substance, and Difference."

*The metaphysical foundation for the new planetary culture is not a world view of matter, of substance, but of pattern*

The metaphysical foundation for the new planetary culture is not a world view of matter, of substance, but of pattern. As Gregory invoked the spirit of Pythagoras, so does Heisenberg, and so do many others. This is the other tradition, the underground tradition, the repressed tradition in Western Civilization, but now that materialism, capitalist and communist, is reaching its limit, we are experiencing "the return of the repressed." So let's go back to this idea of pattern. Yesterday, Lew Balamuth talked about Kirlian photography with Lewis Thomas. He described how you can photograph the energy pattern of a leaf through a certain electrical process. If you cut the leaf in half, then photograph it again, the missing half is still there. Well, what is that thing that isn't there? Now, as soon as I say that, of course, you can hear ringing in your head the **Tao Te Ching**; the purpose of the cup comes from the part which isn't there; thirty spokes converge in the hub of a wheel, but the use of the cart comes from the part which isn't there. Thus, non-being is in being. So there is a kind of geometrical substrate of pure form and pattern which is logically prior to matter. The part of the leaf which isn't there is critically important for its life.

Now if we think about these things, we can see that there is a whole world view and a whole culture which derives from them, a polity as well as a religion. There is a relationship between the way we conceive of our bodies and the way we conceive the body-politic. Rhoda was talking about research done on bio-electrical fields; earlier work was done at Yale by Burr and later by Ravitz and the Pittsburgh Medical School. There are proto-neuronal pathways in the development of the nervous system. In a fetus, when the nerve is developing, before it is really tissue, it's an electrical pathway. It's pure geometry; out of that pure form it draws to itself the material which will constitute the nerve. If you think about the implications of that, you can see that it is the absolute refutation of behaviorism and Skinner. The political extension of Skinnerian thought into behavior modification in schools and clinics is based upon an incorrect episte-mology. The implementation of Skinner into free clinics for the poor in a socialized medicine system by H.E.W. would force an erroneous image of mind and body on the body-politic. So, you see, I don't think Gregory is being hair-splitting or airy-fairy in his fussiness about epistemology. Our hairs will soon stand on end in terror if we don't split a few epistemological hairs with Gregory Bateson. His theory of **mind** is getting at the **heart** of what politics is all about.

Take another fact. (I love the way Lewis Thomas added fact after fact.) In the development of the fetus and its nervous tissue, the efferent nerves develop before the afferent; the pathways that extend the brain into the environment develop before the nerves that report about the environment to the brain. Well, think about that; that's the refutation of stimulus-response. The organism en-counters the environment **on its own terms**. The organism unfolds like a flower, like a dancer extending out and creating the magical space around it. What is the basic unit of information here? It is obviously not a piece of matter; it's the organism plus the en-vironment.

When we come down to the DNA, the basic alphabet of in-formation in the cell, there are four nucleotides, much like the four basic forces in matter, and the fourfold vision in Blake, in Yeats, in Vico, in Jung. What is this fourness that seems to be a program, or a score, for the way things happen? If we take the four nucleotides and assemble them in a table, as Crick did in 1965, that table becomes isomorphic to the **I Ching**, as Gunther Stent has pointed out. Now how is it the case that the structure of information in the cells is isomorphic to the structure of information in the oldest book in the world, a book which in its oral sources goes back into the darkness of time? Once again, in talking about information and consciousness, we're not dealing with a world of matter, but a world of music. We're dealing with a world of ideas, and fourness, the quaternity, is an archetypal idea. Even in the old Newtonian universe we like to caricature as a machine, Newton himself did not describe space mechanistically but said that "space is the sensorium for ideas in the mind of God." I suggest that the fourfold vision is one of these ideas.

If we consider the primacy of pattern in the development of the proto-neuronal pathways or in the table of the nucleotides, it begins to recall us to ancient cosmologies. If we moderns live in a description of reality that is inadequate, it is perfectly valid to reach out and take in all sorts of seemingly alien bits of information in a new vision. In the mystical or theosophical tradition, they speak about the etheric dimension and of how there is a subtle physical body which interacts with etheric forces to build up the health of the tissue. The etheric body is much like the body of meridians in Chinese acupuncture. I feel we are coming to the verge of our scientific understanding of the etheric body.

In theosophy, as it is expressed by writers like David Spangler, there are certain principles called the Laws of Manifestation. An idea exists as pure form, and as pure form it draws to itself in the etheric dimension the physical energies which will bring it into external manifestation. What we have here is the reversal of Marx; first you have an idea and then it draws to it the people and the energies and the material to bring it into the physical form we conventionally call reality. Mystics can see the etheric dimension, just as a Kirlian photograph can record the half of the leaf which isn't there. Mystics can see the seed-forms of things which are going to materialize, and since the space-time of the etheric for them is a valid part of universal processes, they do not limit their definition of reality to the merely physical.

The other day Saul said that there was no planetary mythology yet. But there is on the etheric, and Doris Lessing and Karlheinz Stockhausen are sensitive to that dimension and have given it expression in their work. The planetary mythology is not something off in the future; it is right now, and in a very real sense we are expressing it in this conference. As the Shakers said, "Every force evolves a form." Every idea can attract to itself the matter for its concrescence.

In this concrescence there is a relationship between in-**form**-ation and per-**form**-ance. And here is where I begin to diverge a little from Gregory. In Whitehead's "withness of the body," I feel that we are part of the evolutionary process and that our consciousness of nature is not always, as Gregory said, askew. The consciousness of nature is an event in the history of nature. The way words pulse or the nerves fire is in harmony with the way a bird sings or a spiral nebula unfolds. It is possible to evolve in a form, as John Todd is trying to do. (And here John was addressing himself directly to Gregory by saying, "Here is where conscious purpose comes in, and here is where unconscious process is unfolding.") The universe has created us, an event in its natural history, and so we have to come to terms with our consciousness; and the only way to do that is to feel the edges, to learn the limitations of our consciousness. If we don't come to the edge where conscious and unconscious meet, then we don't really understand the form and shape of consciousness. We begin to understand the nature of consciousness when we come to the perimeter of mind, and one way is through the interval between each heartbeat, each breath.

So I feel there is a performance-quality to reality. History is the performance of myth; the universe is a performance of music. Now in myth and in music what I am arguing for is a Logos in the Plotinian sense. Plotinus talks about the ineffable beyond consciousness, the Father, and the Logos, the intelligibility principle. The Logos is like the grammar of the universe. Remember that metaphor I used in **Passages**? I said that I can't rip God out of the universe to show Him to you to prove that He exists, any more than I can rip the grammar of English out of my mouth to prove that it exists. But the grammar of English is generating every sentence and enabling you to understand every sound. So there is a Grammar of Being, and that Grammar of Being is the Logos. The Logos is the form of all forms. It's the program by which God decides, "Since I did the 3-6-9 universe last time, I'm going to try the 3-5-7 one this time."

And so our cosmology of patterns brings us to the threshold of a theology, and theology takes us back to Gregory's point about freedom. Is there free will or determination? If there are patterns, are they patterns of constraint and control? What is the relationship between constraint and control? What is the measure of our limitations? How free are we? How much does time bind us with each heartbeat?

Imagine God at the creation of the universe. In that pregnant instant of silence before creation, He is thinking to Himself and imagining the various possibilities: "Well, if I create a universe and put this new anomaly, Man, into it, I can correct for it by keeping him under my absolute control. He can always mechanically follow my Will and never deviate from it. But since he is always going to follow my Will, I know how that universe will turn out, so there's no need to go ahead and create it. Now, what happens if I create Man and veil my consciousness from him with **Maya** and give him free will? Now that begins to sound like an interesting universe, for even **I** don't know how that will turn out. And God only knows it's hard to find something where I don't know the ending of the story." So God veils his potency from us; he is not a flasher in a trenchcoat who goes "See!" He's more like a spy in a Pynchon novel, maddeningly everpresent and never seen. But the veiling of divinity in **Maya** gives us our freedom so that we're not blown away by Godhead and can get on with the universal divinity of a unique existence. And yet this freedom introduces the principle of evil. If we are free, then we are free to deviate from the Will of God. Therefore, the universe becomes an interesting play and you can see why God went ahead to create this universe, for it is utterly fascinating. How is it going to work out? So the relationship between humanity and God is very much like an act of love; it is not love unless both are free.

Nevertheless, there are principles of limitation and parameters of restraint. There is a relationship between the freedom of the unmanifest and the falling into form in which you take on the body of time-space and begin to play it out.

There is a Taoist model for this.

The lightning comes as an impulse from outside time-space; as it hits the medium of matter, it encounters resistance, and so it is deflected and it zigs and zags through the resisting medium of the phenomenal world. But this zig-zag, this wave action or pulse of opposites, creates the spin that generates motion. The One is undifferentiated and outside time and space, but the phenomenal world of the many is a binary world of opposites: light and dark, good and evil, masculine and feminine, Yin and Yang. As one looks at this mandala of Yin and Yang, he should see it as the spiraling spin of the macrocosmic nebula and the microcosmic positron. The mandala is an ideogram, and an ideogram is a complex of information existing simultaneously on many levels.

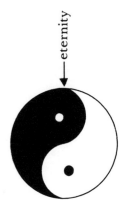

Information is stored in the nature of our cells, in the pulse of the nerves, and so as we watch ourselves think, we can watch a natural event like watching a bird fly or a plant flower. We are observing something that is as valuable and real as any other event in the universe. We do not have to let ourselves fall into the anti-intellectual trap to say, "I'm going to achieve Unity of Being by cutting off my head." The Western attempt to escape the Western mind by sinking into some Lawrencian consciousness of the loins is an exchange of symptoms, not an achievement of health. I agree with Gregory when he says that it is the subtraction of intellect from emotion which is truly monstrous. Mere feeling is a gush; mere abstraction is a lifeless code, a machine language; ideogramic, or hieroglyphic, language is passionate thought; it's not information merely, but music.

Now John Todd identified his work as "Taoist Science." I feel that when he looks at nature in its elegantly simple complexity, he sees ideograms not FORTRAN. John says that in New Alchemy he is trying to move from hardware to information. He wants to move away from capital-intensive machines, which create the polarities of rich and poor, haves and have-nots, to a culture of freely flowing information. As technology becomes surrounded by this flow, it becomes miniaturized, and miniaturization is what the eleven acre New Alchemy farm is all about.

In a sense, we can call this circumambulating flow of information the Noosphere, and the Noosphere of Chardin is what the Theosophists would call "the etheric grid of earth." Imagine the earth as a geodesic sphere, a crystal of triangular facets, surrounding the planet, receiving energy from the sun and translating it into materialization on the physical plane. This crystal is alive, has a consciousness, and is the body of a god, as we are told in ancient cosmologies. So the Noosphere is a planetary consciousness, a single cell in which we are organelles, as Lewis Thomas has described in **The Lives of a Cell**.

Now if you see Chardin's Noosphere, Thomas's planetary cell,

John Todd's alchemical alembic-farm, Spangler's etheric crystal of earth, and you line them up with Nikola Tesla's vision of the world-system of electrical energy flow, then you see an ideogram, or a hieroglyph. Although I'm saying one word at a time, in a linear, incremental sequence, I am trying to express hieroglyphic thought in language by lining up analogy, after analogy, after analogy. I am trying to use English as if it were the ancient Egyptian language, hieroglyphic Maya, or ideogramic Chinese. I am speaking very densely, and this is why sometimes people have trouble understanding me. By the compression and density, I'm trying to turn English into ideograms. (You can see, now, why Joyce and Pound had to come up to the edge of English in **Finnegans Wake** and the **Cantos**.) If you see all these analogies lined up in a mental space, then you can see a different kind of thinking where thought becomes visual and tactile and oral; it becomes sensuous thought, passionate thought. It is not abstract. People who complain that I'm being abstract don't understand. This is a different way. It's not singular to me; there are others who think this way—they all have trouble, too, in being understood. The motivation in thinking this way is that it brings little mind in touch with Big Mind, and in this it resembles art. And that is why yesterday I said with Lewis Thomas that if we're going to deal with information-overload, we're going to have to move out of traditional scholarship into a new kind of art, for scholarship is far too limited.

Now let's go back to the vision of the whole earth and consider the energy theories of Tesla. If energy is everywhere, then you no longer have resources at the periphery pumped to the center. You no longer have capital-intensive economies of scale controlled by elites at the center. You have a hermetic vision of that other Nicholas, Nicholas of Cusa, who described a space in which ''The center is everywhere, the circumference nowhere.'' If any person anywhere on earth can walk into a cabin in the mountains, throw a switch, and have plentiful power, then the microcosm of his domestic unit is relating directly to the macrocosm of the ecosystem of the planet. In a sense, I think some of the things Sean's ''Bioshelter'' is doing are moving in that direction. The hooker in all of this, of course, is the Faustian impulse to beat the whole earth with vibrations so that it gives us all the power we want. There is a pronounced shadow to Tesla, and I am not at all arguing for a simple acceptance.

Nevertheless, Tesla's vision does represent a shift from civilization to planetization, and that is why I am referring to it. What happens when we move to a vision of space in which the center is everywhere and the circumference nowhere? It's not elitist; there are no great accumulations of capital needed to drive economies of scale. There is no need for accumulations of populations in great cities, and no need to control the resources of the periphery from a world city, be that world city Ur or New York. The whole structure of civilization which emerged in Sumeria in the fourth millennium B.C. is transcended. Life becomes a highly "civilized" way of returning to wildness, to "savagery." We become hunters and gatherers again, gatherers of wind and sun. We end up with a Taoist culture of simplicity, not of poverty. Poverty is the linked-opposite of the culture of wealth, and poverty and wealth are the polarities of civilization, not planetization. When we truly move into a vision of a new culture, we will not have to hate wealth and romanticize poverty. I really saw this in India. Better to live with less rather than more; better a cave in the Himalayas as a yogi than an alley in Madras as a worker. Asceticism is a full life of elegance, of clear air, clean water, and open spaces. So the romantic fascination with poverty that many bourgeois student-revolutionaries have is simply a linked-opposite to materialist society. We must not think that the New Age is going to be a culture of poverty. That is a limitation in our thinking, one that, I think, needs to be transcended in the imagining of a wholly new culture.

To imagine a new culture, you have to understand the power of myth. It was the mythology of industrial society which conquered the world with its rags-to-riches legends of universal wealth. People fled the countryside into the cities, for the cities held out to them the prospect of wealth, fame, and power. Never mind the reality of the slums of Manchester, Calcutta, Caracas, New York; the villager was not living in reality, he was living in the Imagination. From Defoe's **Moll Flanders** in the eighteenth century to Podhoretz's **Making It** in the twentieth, the myth of the modern world is fleeing what Marx called "the idiocy of rural life" for the glamour of an opulent life in the cities.

Now that the forests are being turned into Kleenex, now that America has six percent of the world's population consuming thirty percent of the world's resources and producing God only knows how much of the world's pollution, we begin to question the power of the materialist mythology. Industrialization, urbanization, and nationalism: these are the emanations of the myth, and these are the forces which are now at the time of their most dramatic sunset. If we continue to turn forests into Kleenex, if the Amazon valley becomes another Manchester or Pittsburgh or Tokyo, then this colorful sunset is simply human civilization going out in a blaze of glory.

But there is a new planetary mythology emerging and it contains the seed-forms of a wholly new planetary culture. If animism returns and we begin to see that everything is alive, trees and metals, then we will husband our resources to craft an instrument to last for generations. We will move away from heating up the economy through advertizing goods with built-in obsolescence to a craft production of Zen mindfulness. But we don't have to go to Japan to find Zen mindfulness, we can go back to the Shakers. Mother Anne, the founder of the Shakers, said, "Do your work as if it were to last a thousand years and you were to die tomorrow." Goods crafted with Shaker mindfulness are very good indeed. If we reconnect consciousness with craft, and if we reconnect the community with the local ecology, then the familiar world of Detroit and Los Angeles will disappear. If we move from capital-intensive economies of scale to labor-intensive communities of contemplatives, many of the authoritarian solutions for the problems of a dying industrial civilization become unnecessary. If we take Saul Mendlovitz's proposal seriously, that we should do nothing that won't benefit the lower third of humanity, we move in the direction of Gandhi and St. Francis. We move in the direction of a contemplative culture of simplicity.

To change the world we will need to change America first, for America and England are karmically responsible for the mess the world is in. To change the world, we have to listen to it first, the whole earth, not simply the businessmen in Bombay, Osaka, and Tehran: the forests, the oceans, the whales, devas and elementals all.

If we make the transition from industrial to meta-industrial culture, I think we will see a convergence of the thought of Jefferson, Gandhi, and Mao. As we turn on the spiral into meta-industrial culture, we come very close to pre-industrial. As we move from hardware to information, we experience a planetization of the archaic. Lovingly, in a Hegelian **aufheben**, we lift up into ourselves the cultures we have destroyed. This is always the way it is in the dialectic of cultures: the Crusaders invade Islam, and then Islam creates the Renaissance; the English invade Ireland, and then the Protestant Irish create the Irish Literary Renaissance; the whites railroad the Indians, and now we read the **Book of the Hopi** and **Black Elk Speaks**.

The first step in the transition from industrial to meta-industrial is the planetization of the archaic. In the return of yoga, Buddhism, Sufism, Indian Shamanism, and Celtic animism, we surround our old machines with an even older consciousness to experience something wholly novel. As our machines become surrounded, they become miniaturized, for the second step is the miniaturization of technology. As we move from frictional machines of moving parts to solid-state transistors, we shift the scale of man to machine. In the phrase of Pascal, we can say that the trees become great, the machines tiny, and man in just proportion. What makes the miniaturization of technology possible is the expansion of consciousness. The Noosphere now surrounds all the cultures of the earth, and that's why all the cultures of the earth now seem like displays in a museum. In the old industrial culture the technology is based on machines of moving parts which generate work and friction; the polity is based upon moving parties which equally generate work and friction through conflict. The Noosphere is based upon a polity of group meditation in which we move from corporeal to mental war and discover that, as Blake said, ''In opposition is true friendship.'' And so after the planetization of the archaic and the miniaturization of technology comes the resacralization of polity, and politics.

In industrial society an iron wall separates the sacred and the profane; an iron wall separates nature and culture. But as we begin to shift from iron walls to light-permeable membranes, as in Sean's work, we place just such a light-permeable membrane between nature and culture. The Church which constructed its Cathedrals to keep out the pagan forces of nature and to color the light with Bible stories must open again to the spirits of earth, air, fire, and water. The factories which tried to turn Christendom into commerce, to burn the night with gas and darken the day with smoke, must become as quiet and ancient as a stone artifact of another era.

If we put it all together—the epistemology, the metaphysics, the ecology, the economy, the politics—what we have is the resacralization of humanity in an evolving deme, the meta-industrial village. The unit of evolution is the species plus the environment; that unit is the deme in which the mutation has occurred. In the meta-industrial village, the shift from hardware to information will also involve a shift from hierarchical institutions to personal communities. This shift would begin with birth, and Leboyer's ideas in **Birth Without Violence** would introduce the new soul to the community in a contemplative fashion. This move from hospitals to homes for birth would also be true for the end of life, and contemplative birth and death would affirm the sacredness of life. From hospitals to homes, from universities to educational communities, from factories to meta-industrial villages, from churches to the clergy of the laity, from walls to light-permeable membranes: the shift from civilization to planetization is a shift from institutions to individuals.

Planetary culture is post-institutional and anarchic. The center is everywhere and the circumference nowhere. And the energy base which supports that culture is not oil for economies of scale, but solar energy. If we take Gregory's essay on Alcoholics Anonymous, the Gospel according to Gregory again, we can set up another analogy. In that essay he talks about symmetrical and complementary relationships. Now these forms of symmetrical and complementary relationships relate to the role of energy and power in our society. Nuclear power is a symmetrical system; it is an arms race between nations and an arms race in the market system of a consumer society with its economies of scale. Solar power, which uses a gentle respiration of the sun, falls everywhere, and if it does not provide enough energy for a competitive market system, it provides ample energy for a decent culture of universal simplicity. If we are going to shift from post-industrial society, with its nuclear reactors which will kill us, to meta-industrial culture, then we will have to shift from a symmetrical relationship with nature to a complementary one. Gerard

O'Neill with his space colonies is still thinking in a symmetrical fashion. To spend two hundred billion dollars to put a solar collector out in space so that it can beam down concentrations of energy in laser beams is simply to create another weapon in the arms race. It is linear and unimaginative thinking. I'm saying that the paradigm shift is simpler and more elegant, a shift from hardware to information, as John Todd says, a shift away from the factory system and economies of scale.

The political implications of this shift from the corporate systems of post-industrial society to the meta-industrial villages of planetary culture are enormous. With animism and electronics as the polarities of the deme, the culture would appear to be a higher turn on the spiral back to the Jeffersonian agrarian republic. If the information flow, both from esoteric mystical sources and exoteric electronic instruments, can obviate the need for the giantism of institutions, cities, and states, then the form of human governance could be quite light. It would be Taoist and not Confucian; there would be a separation between authority and power, and Gregory Bateson would not be President. Henry Lerner said, "The brightest people and the most powerful should come together to give us enlightened policy management." But I see that as the world we've already had in the political marriage of Harvard and Washington. I'm not arguing for a new planetary theocracy of mystics and Pythagorean scientists in a world-order government; I'm arguing for a Taoist system in which the sage and the emperor are not the same person or in the same government. I'm arguing about the necessity of taking charisma away from the idols of the modern world in nationalism, industrialization, urbanization, and government.

The meta-industrial village of the twenty-first century will have to be Lindisfarne and New Alchemy together: the Grail and the Alembic. With a democratic polity held together by group meditation, and a technology based upon the flow of information through the light-permeable membrane between nature and culture, we would finally realize a harmony between what José has termed **psyche** and **techne, vajra** and **upaya.**

Now it's all well and good to have a vision of a different future, and for that we need ideals, but to have an understanding of the present, we also need to have a vision of evil. We live in the dinosaur days of industrial society, and the dinosaurs don't want anything to change; instead they want to change everything to fit their needs. They want the government to subsidize the auto industry, to field strip the Dakotas, to build pipelines across Alaska and nuclear reactors everywhere, so that we can have more of Detroit, New York, and Los Angeles. If we go on in this way, resisting change and evolution, then the bad news of industrial society will simply kill us. But evolution means good news for a change; it means increasing order as opposed to increasing entropy. However, there is a relationship between the bad news of industrial civilization and the good news of planetary culture. If hot and cold become the same, the engine stops, according to the principles of thermodynamics. Well, if the bad news of our industrial civilization stopped, there would be no energy available for change and transformation. All the things that John or Sean or I would be trying to do would come to a halt. It is the disintegration of industrial society that is creating the integrations of planetary culture. The openness of noise, as Gregory said, creates the possibilities for new signals, new information, new music.

*None of us is creating this mythology; rather, we are creations of this new mythos*

Saul said last night that we need a new mythology and that the difficulty in working toward world order is that there is no mythology. I don't think that's the case. I think the planetary mythology does exist. In a way, John, Sean, Jose, Ty, and I, all men in our mid-thirties, are being cast ashore by this new mythology. In ecology, architecture, art, philosophy, or literature, the mode is mythopoeic and, therefore, disorienting for people who do not think mythopoeically. But I don't think the disorientation you are feeling is any different from the disorientation that gave rise to the riots at the first performance of **Le Sacre du Printemps**. None of us is creating this mythology; rather, we are creations of this new mythos.

Industrial civilization conquered the world through mythology, from the Crystal Palace to Apollo 11. Planetary culture will also spread throughout the world through mythology. This mythology is the foundation for whatever technologies or polities we create with conscious purpose. Now, this conference has been one thing on the level of conscious purpose, but I would point to the entire process of the conference, not what I'm saying, but the entire cultural phenomenology we are experiencing. Notice how something larger than conscious purpose overlights it. Sean comes in right in the middle of it, says things at right angles to the discussion, and yet everything he is working on is synchronistic with the whole. Lewis Thomas comes in for a day, and again everything fits in fantastically, another theme in a more complex orchestration. Obviously, I'm not the composer and didn't write the opera of this conference; perhaps, I'm like a conductor trying to honor the composer with a decent performance. Now if with Zen mindfulness we look at the entire process of the conference to understand how we came to be here, and I mean that like a **koan**—you know, ''What is the face you had before you were born?''—**How did you come to be here?** If you understand that, you will feel the new mythology and understand how the new polity is coming to be here now.

# Acknowledgments

Many people and organizations have contributed, either directly or indirectly, to **Earth's Answer.** Grateful acknowledgment is made to the Lilly Endowment and to the Rockefeller Brothers' Fund for grants which have supported the Lindisfarne conferences and the other work of the Association. The assistance of the Institute for World Order helped make the 1974 conference possible.

The major acknowledgment must be made to the conference speakers themselves, both for making the conferences what they were and for working with us on the preparation of the manuscript. Many of these contributors have become Fellows of the Lindisfarne Association, thus sharing in its creation and continuation.

Other people have offered invaluable support to the overall work of Lindisfarne and to this project. Evelyn Ames, Eva and Lewis Balamuth, Marguerite Cato, Betsy and Harry Hollins, Winthrop Knowlton, James Morton, Pat Frank Nesci, Emily Sellon and Nancy Wilson Ross have been special friends and advisers. Lynne McNabb, Roger Musson and Buz Wyeth have provided encouragement and professional advice about book production. Finally, special thanks is given to Tom Quigley, an employee at John F. Kennedy International Airport, who, for no reason other than kindness, searched through the cargo (crowded with caged monkeys and commissary equipment) of a 747 from London for Baker-roshi's corrected galleys and then, after midnight, drove two hours out of his way to hand-deliver them in time for a deadline.

Harcourt Brace Jovanovich, Inc. kindly gave permission to reprint (on p. 13) part of a poem from E.E. Cummings' **Complete Poems: 1913—1962**, 1972.

**Typography:**   Linda Balamuth, Michael Bristol
**Pasteup:**   Michael Bristol, Janet Planet
**Design:**   Michael Katz
**Photography:**   Nina Hagen (pages 2, 14, 32, 58, 71,
                   72, 122, 141, 142, 184, 189, 190, 206)
**Cover Design:**   Sarah Molholm

All aspects of the making of this book, except for the final
printing, have taken place at Lindisfarne.

N. Haydn Stubbing adapted the drawings opposite the Fore-
word and on pages 31, 43, 95 & 155 from his notebook especially
for **Earth's Answer.**

Gregory Bateson, Paolo Soleri and Sean Wellesley-Miller sup-
plied the drawings within their chapters.

The photograph on page 96 was taken by Hilde Atema
Maingay.

**The Lindisfarne Association**

50 Fishcove Road
Southampton, New York  11968

49 West 20th Street
New York, New York  10011